Healthy Slow Cooker Cookbook for Two

Healthy Slow Cooker Cookbook

for two

100 "Fix-and-Forget" Recipes
for Ready-to-Eat Meals

PAMELA ELLGEN

ROCKRIDGE
PRESS

To my brother Michael, who asked me for a slow cooker cookbook. I hope you enjoy many happy weekends of meal prepping and endless delicious dinners from your slow cooker!

1 Slow Cooker + 1 Timer =

100 Ready-to-Eat Meals for Healthy Living

Healthy Slow Cooker Cookbook for Two invites you to add love and flavor to your meals without spending hours in the kitchen! It offers healthy, flavorful, and ridiculously easy meals for everyone from newlyweds and single parents to busy professionals and empty nesters. All the recipes in this book have been developed to follow these guidelines:

- Ingredients are whole, unprocessed foods that you can easily find in any grocery store.

- Recipes are tailored to suit special diets for a variety of health conditions, including diabetes, heart disease, and obesity.

- Instructions offer substitution tips for people with food allergies or sensitivities.

- Most meals require less than 15 minutes of preparation and at least six hours of cooking time for true "fix-and-forget" slow cooking.

- In addition, there are 14 extra stovetop recipes for quick and easy sides to pair with your meals.

Contents

Introduction 9

one   Easy Meals for Health-Conscious Pairs 11

two   Breakfast & Brunch 21

three   Soups & Stews 37

four   Vegetarian & Vegan Dishes 61

five   Pork & Poultry 79

six   Beef & Lamb 103

seven   Grains & Pasta 121

eight   Quick & Easy Sides 133

Appendix A: Measurement Conversions 149

Appendix B: The Dirty Dozen & The Clean Fifteen 150

References 151

Recipe Index 153

Index 155

Introduction

I have loved cooking for as long as I can remember. Spending hours in the kitchen preparing a gourmet meal was and still is my idea of a good time. When I met my husband, Rich, in college, I put my culinary skills to work and whipped up a batch of chocolate chunk and walnut cookies. That was all it took—he was hooked!

Now, more than a decade later, we're married with two children, and I still enjoy preparing foods infused with love and flavor. Although I rarely have hours to devote to cooking, what I have learned in my years in the kitchen is that long cooking times transform ordinary ingredients into something extraordinary, and the slow cooker is the perfect tool for the job. With a slow cooker, I can prepare succulent meats with fall-off-the-bone consistency and coax amazing flavors from everyday vegetables without ever touching frying pan. And, I can do it without a second thought—just toss the ingredients into the slow cooker, set the timer, and look forward to a healthy and delicious meal.

Early in our relationship, Rich and I watched the documentary *Step into Liquid* and decided that someday we would learn to surf. When we moved to Southern California, that dream became a reality—a passion we share and our standing date whenever we can get a babysitter. After a long day at the beach, I love having a healthy meal for two waiting in my slow cooker. Surfing consumes so much energy, we usually return home absolutely ravenous. I could easily consume all the calories I burned and then some! I love that my slow cooker allows me to simply brush the sand off my feet and sit down to a complete, healthy meal. More importantly, the food is nourishing and satisfying—a winning combination for a healthy body and a healthy relationship.

Whether you use your small slow cooker to prepare meals for you and a significant other or to make a meal and leftovers for yourself, you're going to love these recipes!

one

Easy Meals for Health-Conscious Pairs

Making healthy meals in a slow cooker is the simplest way to get a nutritious and delicious meal on the table with the least amount of effort. It's also good for your waistline, your pocketbook, and your relationships. Foods cooked in a slow cooker—especially the recipes in this book—are often lower in fat, salt, and carbohydrates than meals cooked by other methods. Slow cooked meals you've prepared ahead of time also makes it less tempting to go for greasy takeout at the end of a long day. Bonus—while dinner is simmering in the slow cooker, you can spend your time engaging with the people you love!

Why Slow Cooking Healthy Meals Matters

An entire library of books could be devoted to defining what "healthy" means. The term seems to change with every new study and fad diet. I appreciate Michael Pollan's perspective on the topic. In his book *In Defense of Food*, he succinctly argues that people should eat real food, not too much of it, and mostly plants. The recipes in this book fall in line with this healthy-eating philosophy as follows:

- Ingredients are natural, whole foods without additives, preservatives, food dyes, or artificial anything.

- Refined sugars and hydrogenated oils, which contain trans fats, are not used in any of the recipes. Additionally, few recipes call for oil, keeping added fat to a minimum.

- Salt is used sparingly to keep sodium levels to a minimum. You can also choose to eliminate the salt all together, although the small amounts called for in the recipes are beneficial to the overall flavor of the recipe.

- Most of the recipes contain a variety of fresh vegetables.

Nutrition Labels

Many of the recipes in this book are designed specifically for people with heart disease, diabetes, food allergies and intolerances, or weight loss goals. To help you make informed decisions about your health and the foods you prepare and eat, each recipe features nutrition facts and the following health labels:

HEART HEALTHY

According to the American Heart Association (AHA), saturated fat, trans fat, sodium, red meat, sweets, and sugar-sweetened beverages should be limited in a heart-healthy diet. Instead, the AHA recommends choosing a variety of nutritious foods from all the food groups, which include whole fruits and vegetables, whole grains, low-fat dairy products, lean meats, skinless poultry, fish, nuts and legumes, and vegetable oils. The recipes in this book with the "Heart Healthy" label use these same ingredients and have less than 750 milligrams of sodium and 7 grams of saturated fat.

While coconut oil is high in saturated fat, recipes in this book with coconut in the ingredient list are also labeled "Heart Healthy," as its saturated fat is different from that of animal fat. A study published in the *European e-Journal of Clinical Nutrition and Metabolism* showed that coconut oil can increase good (LDL) cholesterol levels, and decrease total bad (HDL) cholesterol and triglyceride levels, and should therefore reduce the risk of cardiovascular disease.

DIABETES FRIENDLY

According to the Mayo Clinic, a diet for managing diabetes should include healthy, fiber-rich carbohydrates such as whole fruits and vegetables, whole grains, legumes, and nuts. It should also include heart-healthy fish, such as cod, tuna, halibut, and salmon; low-fat dairy products; and "good" fats such as avocados, nuts, olives, and extra-virgin olive oil. The Mayo Clinic also recommends limiting saturated fats, trans fats, cholesterol, sodium, sweets, and sugar-sweetened beverages. The recommended range for carbohydrates in a diabetes friendly diet is 45 to 75 grams per (full) meal depending on gender and state of health. The recipes in this book labeled as "Diabetes Friendly" follow these guidelines and have a maximum amount of 70 grams of carbohydrates.

ALLERGY FRIENDLY

The primary allergens—the "Big 8"—include wheat, dairy, eggs, fish, shellfish, tree nuts, soybeans, and peanuts. Recipes with the "Allergy Friendly" label either do not include any of these top eight allergens or include Substitution Tips to modify them to be free of them. If you have any of these food allergies, be sure to choose ingredients that are made by reliable companies to avoid cross-contamination with allergens.

GLUTEN-FREE

A gluten-free diet is often prescribed to treat celiac disease. Those who suffer from this condition cannot eat gluten, a protein in wheat, barley, and rye, so this diet excludes all foods containing gluten. Recipes with a "Gluten-Free" label in this book either have no ingredients with gluten, or a gluten-free alternative is given in a Tip at the end of the recipe. If you are on a gluten-free diet, be sure to check that you are using gluten-free versions of ingredients such as soy sauce and broth and that products like oats have been processed in a gluten-free environment to avoid cross-contamination.

Slow Cooker Food Safety

While slow cooking is generally safe, and often healthier than oven and stovetop cooking, there are a few food safety concerns associated with using a slow cooker:

- Do not use your slow cooker to prepare dry beans; often the heat does not reach the appropriate temperature to destroy the toxins present in uncooked beans, particularly kidney beans.

- Do not attempt to cook frozen foods in the slow cooker, particularly meat. Food has a "danger zone" of 40°F to 140°F, in which bacteria multiply rapidly. In a slow cooker, frozen food does not pass through the danger zone quickly enough to kill these bacteria.

- Do not leave food in your slow cooker in the danger zone temperature range before or after cooking for extended periods of time. The USDA recommends not leaving cold food or cooked food at room temperature for longer than two hours.

- Do not put the slow cooker crock in the refrigerator; a cold crock takes longer to heat up and will compromise food safety.

LOW CALORIE

Recipes that feature the "Low Calorie" label contain 600 or fewer calories per serving, and many of them are between 300 and 400 calories per serving. That means even when you serve them with one of the side dish recipes in this book, the calorie count still remains low. That makes these "Low Calorie" dishes perfect for those keeping an eye on their waistline.

The guidelines for these nutrition labels often overlap. Ultimately, if you're following a specific diet prescribed by a physician, be sure to follow their advice about what you should eat.

Health Benefits of Using a Slow Cooker

Slow cooking does not usually require added fat to prevent food from sticking to the surface of the cooking vessel. The slow cooking process accentuates the complex flavors of vegetables and herbs so you can use less salt. Additionally, the lower cooking temperatures of a slow cooker reduce nutrient loss. Cooking at low temperatures also prevents the formation of advanced glycation end-products (AGEs) caused by cooking certain foods, particularly proteins, at very high heat. According to a study published in the *Journal of the American Dietetic Association*, AGEs may contribute to diabetes, heart disease, and Alzheimer's disease. So, you could say, slow cooking is good for your heart and mind!

Smart Planning for Slow Cooker Success

My favorite slow cooker is a no-frills, 1.5-quart-capacity machine with only two settings, low and high. It easily makes enough food for me and my husband and two portions more for our small children. The recipes in this book have been developed with this inexpensive model in mind, so you needn't worry about the advanced functions of more expensive models.

You can use a 1.5-quart or 2-quart slow cooker for the recipes in this book. Alternately, if you already own a 4-quart slow cooker or need to cook for more than two people, simply double the recipe ingredients, with the exception of the liquids, which are only increased by half, and use the longer cooking time if one is suggested.

Choosing a Slow Cooker

Some slow cookers have a variety of helpful features, though none are essential for the recipes in this book. Some of these "bells and whistles" include:

- A locking lid to ensure no heat escapes and allow for portability.

- A programmable timer to set the cooking time. Many have a preset function that switches the heat setting to warm after the cooking time has elapsed.

- Built-in thermometers to check the internal temperature of the dish while leaving the lid in place.

Using a Socket Timer

If you do not have a slow cooker with a timer and a warming setting, you may wish to invest in a socket timer to allow for shorter cooking times if you're away from your kitchen for longer than the recommended cooking time. Plug the timer into the wall socket and the slow cooker into the timer, with the timer set as needed. For example, if the cooking time specified is eight hours but you will be away from home for ten hours, set the timer to start cooking one hour after you depart and shut off one hour before you return. According to the USDA, it is safe to leave cooked food in a slow cooker that has been turned off for up to two hours. The food can then be reheated on the stovetop or in the microwave before serving.

Planning Ahead

Many of the recipe preparation steps can be completed the night before and the ingredients stored in the refrigerator. The next morning, put them into the slow cooker crock (remember that the crock should never be kept in the refrigerator) and place the crock into the slow cooker base. Set your timer and be on your way.

Tips & Tricks for Delicious, Healthy, Slow Cooked Meals

Cooking food in a slow cooker is similar to stovetop cooking, with a few key differences. There are helpful tips you can follow to ensure enticing meals from your slow cooker.

1. Due to long cooking times, some foods, especially starchy vegetables, can turn to mush in the slow cooker. Layer ingredients, putting those that benefit from longer cooking times, such as tough cuts of meat, on the bottom of the slow cooker with the liquid and placing tender vegetables at the top.

2. Woody herbs, such as rosemary and thyme, can be added at the beginning of cooking. Fragile fresh herbs, such as basil and cilantro, should be stirred in just prior to serving. Dried herbs of all varieties should be added at the beginning of the cooking time.

3. When doubling recipes, add only half of the second portion of liquid called for. For example, when making a recipe for beef stew that calls for 1 quart of beef broth, use 1.5 quarts when you double the recipe.

4. Do not cook meats with fresh raw pineapple in the slow cooker. The enzymes in the fruit break down the proteins in the meat, and will turn it to an unappetizing mush. The enzyme in fresh pineapple is denatured during the canning (cooking) process, so canned pineapple is acceptable to use in slow cooking.

5. If you're watching your dietary fat intake, choose lean cuts of meat. The meat can then be cooked on the stovetop and the rendered fat drained before the meat is added to the slow cooker. Because fat rises to the top of liquids, an alternative step is to cook the meat in the slow cooker and later skim the fat from the top with a spoon.

6. None of the recipes in this book rely on bottled sauces or soup packets for flavor. Be sure to choose the best quality ingredients you can find.

7. If you use frozen ingredients, make sure to thaw them completely under cool running water before adding them to the slow cooker.

8. As tempting as it may be, do not remove the lid from your slow cooker during the cooking process. If you are near the end of cooking and want to check for doneness, do so quickly and replace the lid immediately. Removing the lid during cooking allows heat to escape and increases the total cooking time.

9. Do not over- or under-fill the slow cooker; aim for filling the crock about three-quarters full for optimal cooking.

Healthy Ingredients for a Healthier You

Fresh food picked in season not only tastes better, it is also better for you. Consider a fresh tomato picked from the vine in the warm summer sunshine. It is bursting with flavor and nutrients. If you've ever tried mushroom soup made from scratch with wild mushrooms and thickened with a good roux, you know how superior it tastes to the soup that comes in a can.

As a general rule, choose fresh, organic, in-season produce whenever possible and use it shortly after purchase. You may also find you prefer the flavor and nutritional quality of grass-fed and pastured animal products.

Certain foods do better in a slow cooker than others. Water-rich fruits such as strawberries, raspberries, and watermelon break down quickly in the slow cooker. So, too, do delicate greens such as lettuce. Pasta is tricky in a slow cooker because it easily becomes mushy.

Some fruits and vegetables may be "in season" for nearly half the year, depending on where you live. The following is a brief guide to slow cooker–friendly ingredients to prepare in each season:

Spring	Summer	Fall	Winter
Asparagus	Apricots	Acorn squash	Brussels sprouts
Broccoli	Beets	Apple	Celeriac
Cabbage	Eggplant	Butternut squash	Collard greens
Fennel	Green beans	Cauliflower	Escarole
Peas	Peaches	Mushrooms	Kale
Mustard greens	Peppers	Pears	Leeks
Spinach	Tomatillos	Pumpkin	Parsnips
Swiss chard	Zucchini	Sweet potatoes	Turnips

Shopping and Storage Tips

Following are a few methods to help you shop wisely, save money, and keep food fresher longer.

SHOP WITH A LIST

You may typically plan five or six dinners for each week assuming that one or more nights will be dinner with friends, on the go, or leftovers. Shopping with a list ensures you are never faced with the dinnertime dilemma of what to cook and a last-minute dash to the market.

BUY IN BULK

Dry foods such as nuts and beans can often be purchased in bulk the bulk bins. The exception to this is if you find a store that carries packaged nuts for slightly lower prices and has high shelf turnover for the freshest food possible. If gluten or allergens are a problem, make sure to purchase pre-packaged items that in bulk may be susceptible to cross-contamination, such as gluten-free oats.

STORE INGREDIENTS WISELY

- Store onions, shallots, and garlic separately from root vegetables such as potatoes and sweet potatoes; these foods accelerate spoilage when stored together.

- Store fresh herbs such as cilantro and parsley in the refrigerator, in a glass of water, with a plastic bag as a "tent" over the top. You will be amazed how long they last!

- Store ginger root uncovered at room temperature. It keeps well in a basket with the onions and garlic.

- Keep celery and carrots in a covered container or zip-top bag to prevent them from going limp.

- Store milk and eggs in the main compartment of the refrigerator, not in the door. All of that opening and closing contributes to earlier spoilage.

Now that you have your healthy and delicious ingredients and your slow cooker is off the shelf, it's time to get slow cooking.

two

Breakfast & Brunch

22 Cinnamon Raisin
Steel-Cut Oatmeal

23 Pear Chai-Spiced Oatmeal

24 Pumpkin Spice Oatmeal

25 Breakfast Quinoa & Fruit

26 Cherry-Studded
Quinoa Porridge

27 Strawberry Cream Cheese
French Toast

28 Banana Nut French Toast

29 Yogurt with Mangos &
Cardamom

30 Yogurt & Berry Parfait

31 Southwest Sweet Potato
& Corn Scramble

32 Smoked Salmon &
Potato Casserole

33 Prosciutto, Rosemary &
Potato Breakfast Casserole

34 Ham & Cheese
Breakfast Casserole

35 Southwest Breakfast Casserole

HEART
HEALTHY

DIABETES
FRIENDLY

ALLERGY
FRIENDLY

GLUTEN-
FREE

LOW
CALORIE

PREP
5 minutes

COOK
8 hours

PER SERVING
Calories: 293
Saturated Fat: 1g
Trans Fat: 0g
Carbohydrates: 56g
Fiber: 7g
Sodium: 132mg
Protein: 10g

Cinnamon Raisin Steel-Cut Oatmeal

Serves 2

Steel-cut oats are whole-grain oat groats that have been chopped into bits about the size of a pinhead. When used to make oatmeal, they provide a slightly smoother consistency than rolled oats with all the fiber and nutrients in the whole grain. Steel-cut oats are rich in protein, fiber, and iron, making them a healthy, filling breakfast to wake up to.

¾ cup steel-cut oats

¼ cup raisins

1 teaspoon ground cinnamon

⅛ teaspoon sea salt

3 cups almond milk or water

1. Put the oats, raisins, cinnamon, and salt in the slow cooker and stir to combine. Pour in the almond milk and stir.

2. Cover and cook the oatmeal on low for 8 hours or overnight.

SUBSTITUTION TIP To ensure this recipe is Gluten-Free, use gluten-free steel-cut oats from a trusted brand, and to make it Allergy Friendly, use the water instead of the almond milk.

Pear Chai-Spiced Oatmeal

Serves 2

HEART
HEALTHY

DIABETES
FRIENDLY

ALLERGY
FRIENDLY

GLUTEN-
FREE

LOW
CALORIE

The aromas and flavors of chai can be especially satisfying on chilly autumn mornings. Unfortunately, many chai-inspired recipes contain a lot of sugar and full-fat milk. This chai-spiced oatmeal is sweetened naturally with diced pear and has a creamy texture from the almond milk.

¾ cup steel-cut oats

⅛ teaspoon ground cardamom

⅛ teaspoon ground nutmeg

⅛ teaspoon ground ginger

¼ teaspoon cinnamon

⅛ teaspoon sea salt

1 ripe pear, cored, peeled, and diced

3 cups unsweetened almond milk or water

PREP
5 minutes

COOK
8 hours

1. Put the oats, cardamom, nutmeg, ginger, cinnamon, and salt in the slow cooker and stir to combine. Stir in the pear and the almond milk.

2. Cover and cook the oatmeal on low for 8 hours or overnight.

NUTRITION TIP A study published by the American Diabetes Association showed that cinnamon may lower blood glucose and lipid profiles in people with type 2 diabetes, offering yet another reason to add the sweet spice to your morning meal.

SUBSTITUTION TIP To ensure this recipe is Gluten-Free, use gluten-free steel-cut oats from a trusted brand, and to make it Allergy Friendly, use the water instead of the almond milk.

PER SERVING
Calories: 323
Saturated Fat: 1g
Trans Fat: 0g
Carbohydrates: 53g
Fiber: 10g
Sodium: 343mg
Protein: 11g

HEART
HEALTHY

DIABETES
FRIENDLY

ALLERGY
FRIENDLY

GLUTEN-
FREE

LOW
CALORIE

PREP
5 minutes

COOK
8 hours

PER SERVING
Calories: 310
Saturated Fat: 1g
Trans Fat: 0g
Carbohydrates: 52g
Fiber: 13g
Sodium: 273mg
Protein: 12g

Pumpkin Spice Oatmeal

Serves 2

Every fall pumpkin-spiced everything seems to fill restaurant menus and social media sites. Like chai spice–flavored foods, many of these foods are loaded with sugar as well as refined flour and fat. However, that's no reason to ignore the trend altogether. Instead, savor it in this healthy pumpkin oatmeal.

¾ cup steel-cut oats

1 teaspoon ground cinnamon

⅛ teaspoon ground ginger

⅛ teaspoon ground nutmeg

⅛ teaspoon ground cloves

⅛ teaspoon sea salt

1 cup pumpkin purée

2 cups unsweetened almond milk or water

1. Combine the oats, cinnamon, ginger, nutmeg, cloves, and salt in the slow cooker.

2. In a medium bowl, whisk together the pumpkin and almond milk and pour the mixture into the oats. Stir gently to combine the ingredients.

3. Cover and cook the oatmeal on low for 8 hours or overnight.

NUTRITION TIP Pumpkin is rich in vitamins A, C, E, and K and the minerals iron, magnesium, potassium, manganese, and copper, making this dish tasty and nutritious.

SUBSTITUTION TIP To ensure this recipe is Gluten-Free, use gluten-free steel-cut oats from a trusted brand, and to make it Allergy Friendly, use the water instead of the almond milk.

Breakfast Quinoa & Fruit

Serves 2

I like to use red quinoa for this recipe for a change of texture and color. The options for fruit are nearly endless. You can use frozen fruit (defrost it first), fresh fruit, dehydrated fruit, or even canned fruit in a pinch.

¾ cup quinoa

2 cups fresh fruit

⅛ teaspoon sea salt

1 teaspoon vanilla extract

3 cups water

2 tablespoons toasted pecans, for garnish

1. Put the quinoa, fruit, and salt in the slow cooker. Add in the vanilla extract and water, and mix thoroughly.

2. Cover and cook on low for 8 hours or overnight.

3. Garnish each serving with a sprinkle of the toasted pecans.

VARIATION TIP For a unique twist, add a couple of drops of almond or lemon oil in addition to the vanilla extract.

PREP
5 minutes

COOK
8 hours

PER SERVING
Calories: 323
Saturated Fat: 1g
Trans Fat: 0g
Carbohydrates: 53g
Fiber: 8g
Sodium: 122mg
Protein: 11g

HEART
HEALTHY

DIABETES
FRIENDLY

ALLERGY
FRIENDLY

GLUTEN-
FREE

LOW
CALORIE

PREP
5 minutes

COOK
8 hours

PER SERVING
Calories: 426
Saturated Fat: 0g
Trans Fat: 0g
Carbohydrates: 78g
Fiber: 16g
Sodium: 352mg
Protein: 12g

Cherry-Studded
Quinoa Porridge

Serves 2

Quinoa is a grain-like seed that swells when cooked and has a texture similar to brown rice. It is packed with protein, making it a healthy, vegan alternative to eggs for breakfast. Quinoa is also a great source of fiber, which slows the absorption of sugar and starches and helps you feel full for longer.

¾ cup quinoa

½ cup dried cherries

⅛ teaspoon sea salt

1 teaspoon vanilla extract

3 cups almond milk or water

1. Put the quinoa, cherries, and salt in the slow cooker. Pour in the vanilla and almond milk, and stir all of the ingredients together.

2. Cover and cook on low for 8 hours or overnight.

VARIATION TIP Top this porridge with a drizzle of coconut oil and a sprinkle of toasted pecan pieces to add some healthy fat and protein.

SUBSTITUTION TIP To ensure this porridge is Allergy Friendly, cook the oatmeal with water instead of the almond milk.

Strawberry Cream Cheese French Toast

Serves 2

The slow cooker provides the perfect cooking vessel for moist French toast. If you can find artisan whole-grain bread, the taste and texture it adds is worth the splurge. This recipe can also be made with your favorite gluten-free bread. The strawberries add plenty of sweetness, but feel free to add a drizzle of maple syrup if you wish when serving.

PREP
10 minutes

COOK
6 hours on low,
2½ hours on high

PER SERVING
Calories: 391
Saturated Fat: 10g
Trans Fat: 0g
Carbohydrates: 40g
Fiber: 7g
Sodium: 606mg
Protein: 17g

1 teaspoon butter, at room temperature

2 eggs

½ cup 2% milk

1 teaspoon vanilla extract

⅛ teaspoon sea salt

4 slices whole-grain bread, crusts removed, cut into 1-inch cubes

2 cups fresh strawberries

2 ounces low-fat cream cheese, cut into small chunks

1. Grease the inside of the slow cooker with the butter.

2. In a large bowl, whisk together the eggs, milk, vanilla, and salt. Toss the bread cubes in this mixture until they are thoroughly saturated.

3. Pour half of the bread mixture into the slow cooker. Top with the strawberries and cream cheese. Add the remaining bread mixture.

4. Cover and cook on low for 6 hours or on high for 2½ hours. To prepare the dish the night before, set a timer to turn on the slow cooker (set on low) one hour after you go to bed and turn off one hour before you plan to eat breakfast, for a total cook time of 6 hours.

SUBSTITUTION TIP If strawberries aren't in season, consider using peeled and diced apples, pears, or another seasonal fruit. Do not use frozen fruit; it will keep the dish in the temperature danger zone for too long and slow the cooking process.

HEART
HEALTHY

DIABETES
FRIENDLY

LOW
CALORIE

PREP
10 minutes

COOK
4 hours on low,
2 hours on high

PER SERVING
Calories: 423
Saturated Fat: 5g
Trans Fat: 0g
Carbohydrates: 59g
Fiber: 9g
Sodium: 537mg
Protein: 17g

Banana Nut French Toast

Serves 2

This recipe has the taste of pure decadence but without the sugar and fat you might expect. I prefer to use freshly ground nutmeg. Purchase a whole nutmeg and run it over a microplane grater. The fragrance is intoxicating!

1 teaspoon butter, at room temperature

2 eggs

¾ cup 2% milk

1 teaspoon vanilla extract

1 teaspoon ground cinnamon

¼ teaspoon ground nutmeg

⅛ teaspoon sea salt

2 cups sliced bananas

4 slices whole-grain bread, crusts removed, cut into 1-inch cubes

2 tablespoons finely chopped toasted pecans

1. Grease the inside of the slow cooker with the butter.

2. In a large bowl, whisk together the eggs, milk, vanilla, cinnamon, nutmeg, and salt. Gently toss the bananas and bread cubes in the mixture until the bread is thoroughly saturated.

3. Pour the bread and banana mixture into the slow cooker. Sprinkle the top with the toasted pecans.

4. Cover and cook on low for 4 hours or on high for 2 hours.

SERVING TIP For a full brunch, enjoy this casserole with a steaming cup of coffee, a few slices of bacon, and a piece of fresh fruit.

Yogurt with Mangos & Cardamom

Serves 4

This is a riff on the Indian yogurt-based mango lassi beverage. It can be served as a parfait or blended into a smoothie. If you do not have access to fresh mangos, you can purchase jarred mangos and use some of the syrup from the jar in place of the honey.

4 cups 2% milk

¼ cup plain yogurt with live cultures

2 mangos, cut into chunks

1 tablespoon honey

¼ teaspoon ground cardamom

1. Pour the milk into the slow cooker. Cover and cook on low for 2 hours.

2. Unplug the slow cooker and stir in the yogurt. Cover with the lid and wrap the outside of the slow cooker housing with a bath towel to help insulate it. Allow it to rest for 8 hours or overnight.

3. For a thick yogurt, strain the mixture in a medium bowl through a few layers of cheesecloth for 10 to 15 minutes. Discard the whey remaining in the cheesecloth or save it for making smoothies.

4. To serve, stir in the mango chunks, honey, and cardamom. Refrigerate leftovers.

VARIATION TIP To make a protein smoothie, add the cooked yogurt to a blender with the mango, honey, cardamom, a scoop of protein powder, and 2 cups of crushed ice. Blend until creamy.

PREP
5 minutes

COOK
10 hours

PER SERVING
Calories: 206
Saturated Fat: 3g
Trans Fat: 0g
Carbohydrates: 31g
Fiber: 2g
Sodium: 128mg
Protein: 9g

HEART
HEALTHY

DIABETES
FRIENDLY

LOW
CALORIE

PREP
5 minutes

COOK
10 hours

PER SERVING
Calories: 266
Saturated Fat: 4g
Trans Fat: 0g
Carbohydrates: 44g
Fiber: 4g
Sodium: 183mg
Protein: 11g

Yogurt & Berry Parfait

Serves 4

Be sure to start the yogurt in the afternoon or evening so that it can rest overnight. This recipe yields four servings, giving you breakfast for two on two separate mornings. Store the leftovers for the second breakfast in separate tightly sealed containers in the refrigerator.

4 cups 2% milk

¼ cup plain yogurt with live cultures

2 cups blueberries

1 cup low-fat, low-sugar granola

1. Pour the milk into the slow cooker. Cover and cook on low for 2 hours.

2. Unplug the slow cooker and stir in the yogurt. Put the lid on and wrap the slow cooker in a bath towel to help insulate it. Allow the yogurt to rest for 8 hours or overnight.

3. For a thick yogurt, strain the mixture into a medium bowl through a few layers of cheesecloth for 10 to 15 minutes. Discard the whey remaining in the cheesecloth or save it for making smoothies.

4. To serve, layer the strained yogurt with the berries and the granola.

VARIATION TIP For a dairy-free alternative, use almond or coconut milk. Omit the yogurt and purchase a starter culture designed for use with non-dairy milk, such as vegan yogurt starter culture, and follow the instructions on the package.

Southwest Sweet Potato & Corn Scramble

Serves 2

This was the first overnight breakfast recipe I made in my slow cooker. Coming home to a hot meal in the evening is delightful, but waking up to a hot breakfast is even better. It is especially wonderful on busy school mornings.

PREP
10 minutes

COOK
8 hours

1 teaspoon butter, at room temperature, or extra-virgin olive oil

4 eggs

½ cup 2% milk

⅛ teaspoon sea salt

½ teaspoon smoked paprika

½ teaspoon ground cumin

Freshly ground black pepper

1 cup finely diced sweet potato

1 cup frozen corn kernels, thawed

½ cup diced roasted red peppers

2 tablespoons minced onion

PER SERVING
Calories: 349
Saturated Fat: 5g
Trans Fat: 0g
Carbohydrates: 45g
Fiber: 6g
Sodium: 430mg
Protein: 18g

1. Grease the inside of the slow cooker with the butter.

2. In a small bowl, whisk together the eggs, milk, salt, paprika, and cumin. Season with the freshly ground black pepper.

3. Put the sweet potato, corn, red pepper, and onion into the slow cooker. Pour in the egg mixture and stir gently.

4. Cover and cook on low for 8 hours or overnight.

SUBSTITUTION TIP To make this dairy-free, use the olive oil to grease the crock and unsweetened coconut milk instead of dairy milk.

PREP
10 minutes

COOK
8 hours

PER SERVING
Calories: 355
Saturated Fat: 5g
Trans Fat: 0g
Carbohydrates: 40g
Fiber: 5g
Sodium: 1397mg
Protein: 24g

Smoked Salmon & Potato Casserole

Serves 2

As a Northwest native, I have enjoyed smoked salmon since I was a child. The delicacy is usually set out at room temperature before serving, but the smoky, salty flavor of the salmon cooked in this casserole and served hot, it is a real treat!

1 teaspoon butter, at room temperature, or extra-virgin olive oil

2 eggs

1 cup 2% milk

1 teaspoon dried dill

⅛ teaspoon sea salt

Freshly ground black pepper

2 medium russet potatoes, peeled and sliced thin

4 ounces smoked salmon

1. Grease the inside of the slow cooker with the butter.

2. In a small bowl, whisk together the eggs, milk, dill, salt, and a few grinds of the black pepper.

3. Spread one-third of the potatoes in a single layer on the bottom of the slow cooker and top them with one-third of the salmon. Pour one-third of the egg mixture over the salmon. Repeat this layering with the remaining potatoes, salmon, and egg mixture.

4. Cover and cook on low for 8 hours or overnight.

NUTRITION TIP Salmon is rich in omega-3 fatty acids, which decrease the risk of arrhythmias, decrease triglyceride levels, slow the growth of atherosclerotic plaque, and slightly lower blood pressure.

Prosciutto, Rosemary & Potato Breakfast Casserole

Serves 2

The combination of rosemary and prosciutto works in everything from tapas to eggs. Purchase or pick fresh rosemary if you can. When dried, the herb loses its heady aroma and is too dry and woody in texture.

1 teaspoon butter, at room temperature, or extra-virgin olive oil

4 eggs

½ cup 2% milk

1 tablespoon minced fresh rosemary

⅛ teaspoon sea salt

Freshly ground black pepper

2 medium russet potatoes, peeled and sliced thin

2 ounces prosciutto

PREP
10 minutes

COOK
8 hours

PER SERVING
Calories: 367
Saturated Fat: 5g
Trans Fat: 0g
Carbohydrates: 39g
Fiber: 6g
Sodium: 637mg
Protein: 23g

1. Grease the inside of the slow cooker with the butter.

2. In a small bowl, whisk together the eggs, milk, rosemary, salt, and a few grinds of the black pepper.

3. Layer one-third of the potatoes in bottom of the slow cooker and top that layer with one-third of the prosciutto. Pour one-third of the egg mixture over the prosciutto. Repeat this layering with the remaining ingredients.

4. Cover and cook on low for 8 hours or overnight.

NUTRITION TIP Prosciutto has all the smoky scrumptiousness of bacon, but less than half of the calories and fat.

PREP
10 minutes

COOK
8 hours

PER SERVING
Calories: 324
Saturated Fat: 8g
Trans Fat: 0g
Carbohydrates: 19g
Fiber: 5g
Sodium: 866mg
Protein: 27g

Ham & Cheese
Breakfast Casserole

Serves 2

Choose a good-quality aged ham, such as Jamón Serrano, to enrich the flavor of this breakfast casserole. The Parmesan cheese in this recipe is rich in protein and calcium, but can be substituted with Manchego cheese, which is made with sheep's milk, for a mellower taste treat.

1 teaspoon butter, at room temperature, or extra-virgin olive oil

2 eggs

2 egg whites

Freshly ground black pepper

2 slices whole-grain bread, crusts removed, cut into 1-inch cubes

2 ounces aged ham, diced

2 ounces hard cheese, such as Parmesan, shredded

1. Grease the inside of the slow cooker with the butter.

2. In a small bowl, whisk together the eggs, egg whites, and a few grinds of the black pepper.

3. Put the bread, ham, and cheese in the slow cooker. Pour the egg mixture over the top and stir gently to combine.

4. Cover and cook on low for 8 hours or overnight.

NUTRITION TIP Because both ham and cheese tend to have a lot of sodium, wait until serving to season the casserole with salt.

Southwest Breakfast Casserole

Serves 2

Smoked paprika provides subtle heat and a warm smokiness. With cumin as its trusty sidekick, the two spices bring depth and flavor to this hearty breakfast. The finished casserole is especially great with a drizzle of salsa verde and a dollop of sour cream.

1 teaspoon butter, at room temperature, or extra-virgin olive oil

2 eggs

2 egg whites

1 teaspoon ground cumin

1 teaspoon smoked paprika

⅛ teaspoon sea salt

Freshly ground black pepper

½ cup shredded pepper Jack cheese

½ cup canned fire-roasted diced tomatoes

½ cup canned black beans, drained and rinsed

1 teaspoon minced garlic

3 corn tortillas

¼ cup fresh cilantro, for garnish

PREP
10 minutes

COOK
8 hours

PER SERVING
Calories: 366
Saturated Fat: 9g
Trans Fat: 0g
Carbohydrates: 31g
Fiber: 8g
Sodium: 640mg
Protein: 24g

1. Grease the inside of the slow cooker with the butter.

2. In a small bowl, whisk together the eggs, egg whites, cumin, paprika, salt, and a few grinds of the black pepper.

3. In a separate small bowl, combine the cheese, tomatoes, black beans, and garlic.

4. Place one of the corn tortillas in the slow cooker and top it with half of the cheese and bean mixture. Pour one-third of the egg mixture over the top of the cheese and beans. Top the egg mixture with another tortilla. Top that tortilla with the remaining cheese and bean mixture, followed by one-third of the egg mixture. Place the last tortilla on top of the egg mixture, and then pour the remaining egg mixture over the top of it.

5. Cover and cook on low for 8 hours or overnight. Garnish with the fresh cilantro before serving.

SUBSTITUTION TIP To reduce calories while retaining protein, swap two of the whole eggs with three additional egg whites.

three

Soups & Stews

38   Ginger Carrot Bisque

39   Creamy Butternut Squash
      & Parsnip Soup

40   Mushroom Soup

41   Cream of Fennel & Leek Soup

42   Sweet Spiced Lentil Soup

43   Split Pea Soup

44   Rosemary Parsnip Bisque
      with Toasted Bread Crumbs

45   Corn & Red Pepper Chowder

46   Rutabaga & Sweet Potato Soup
      with Garlicky Ground Walnuts

47   Baked Potato Soup

48   Minestrone

49   Chipotle Black Bean Soup

50   Red Curry
      Butternut Squash Soup

51   Corn & Potato Chowder

52   Vegetable Curry Soup

53   Pumpkin Black Bean Chili

54   Chicken Noodle Soup

55   Garlicky Chicken Kale Soup

56   Chicken Fajita Soup

57   Beef Barley Soup

58   Lentil, Chickpea &
      White Bean Stew

59   Spicy Mediterranean
      Beef Stew with Pearl Barley

HEART
HEALTHY

DIABETES
FRIENDLY

ALLERGY
FRIENDLY

GLUTEN-
FREE

LOW
CALORIE

PREP
10 minutes

COOK
8 hours

PER SERVING
Calories: 226
Saturated Fat: 4g
Trans Fat: 0g
Carbohydrates: 38g
Fiber: 7g
Sodium: 289mg
Protein: 6g

Ginger Carrot Bisque

Serves 2

The ginger and tangy lime juice give this creamy soup a surprising zing. If you prefer a low-fat and dairy-free version, omit the heavy cream.

½ cup diced onion

¼ cup diced celery

1 tablespoon minced ginger

2 cups low-sodium chicken broth

2 cups diced carrots

1 white potato, peeled and diced

1 teaspoon curry powder

⅛ teaspoon sea salt

1 tablespoon freshly squeezed lime juice

2 tablespoons heavy cream (optional)

¼ cup roughly chopped fresh cilantro

1. Put the onion, celery, ginger, broth, carrots, potato, curry powder, and salt in the slow cooker and stir to combine. Cover and cook on low for 8 hours.

2. Add the lime juice to the slow cooker and purée the bisque with an immersion blender.

3. Swirl in the heavy cream (if using) just before serving. Garnish each bowl with the cilantro.

NUTRITION TIP Ginger alleviates digestive discomfort, is a rich source of antioxidants, and has anti-inflammatory effects.

SUBSTITUTION TIP To ensure the soup is Gluten-Free, use gluten-free low-sodium chicken broth. To ensure the soup is Allergy Friendly, omit the cream as well.

Creamy Butternut Squash & Parsnip Soup

Serves 2

HEART
HEALTHY

DIABETES
FRIENDLY

GLUTEN-
FREE

LOW
CALORIE

The sweet tartness of apples pairs beautifully with savory, rich ingredients. This comforting soup goes well with Whole-Grain Dinner Rolls (page 145) and Simple Salad (page 134).

2 cups peeled, diced butternut squash

1 cup peeled, diced parsnip

1 Granny Smith apple, cored, peeled, and diced

½ cup diced onion

⅛ teaspoon sea salt

2 cups low-sodium vegetable broth

1 sprig fresh thyme

1 tablespoon heavy cream

PREP
10 minutes

COOK
8 hours

PER SERVING
Calories: 179
Saturated Fat: 2g
Trans Fat: 0g
Carbohydrates: 38g
Fiber: 5g
Sodium: 192mg
Protein: 3g

1. Put the butternut squash, parsnip, apple, onion, salt, vegetable broth, and thyme into the slow cooker and stir to combine.

2. Cover and cook on low for 8 hours. Remove the thyme sprig and stir in the heavy cream.

3. Use an immersion blender to purée the soup until smooth.

COOKING TIP To save time, purchase precut butternut squash in the refrigerated portion of the produce section.

SUBSTITUTION TIP To ensure the soup is Gluten-Free, use gluten-free low-sodium vegetable broth.

HEART
HEALTHY

DIABETES
FRIENDLY

GLUTEN-
FREE

LOW
CALORIE

PREP
10 minutes

COOK
8 hours

PER SERVING
Calories: 158
Saturated Fat: 4g
Trans Fat: 0g
Carbohydrates: 14g
Fiber: 2g
Sodium: 203mg
Protein: 7g

Mushroom Soup

Serves 2

Dried wild mushrooms add a complex umami flavor to this soup. You can usually find them in the bulk spice section or international food aisle of most markets. Shiitake mushrooms are also a good choice if you cannot find wild mushrooms.

1 ounce dried wild mushrooms

8 ounces cremini mushrooms, washed and quartered

2 cups low-sodium chicken broth

2 tablespoons dry sherry (optional)

1 onion, halved, cut into thin half circles

2 garlic cloves, minced

1 teaspoon fresh thyme

½ teaspoon minced fresh rosemary

⅛ teaspoon sea salt

¼ cup heavy cream

1. Put the wild mushrooms, cremini mushrooms, broth, sherry (if using), onion, garlic, thyme, rosemary, and salt in the slow cooker and stir to combine.

2. Cover and cook on low for 8 hours.

3. Stir in the heavy cream just before serving.

VARIATION TIP For even more flavor, heat 1 tablespoon butter in a large skillet over medium-high heat. Add the fresh mushrooms and brown them for about 2 minutes on each side before adding them to the slow cooker.

SUBSTITUTION TIP To ensure the soup is Gluten-Free, use gluten-free low-sodium chicken broth.

Cream of Fennel & Leek Soup

Serves 2

HEART HEALTHY

DIABETES FRIENDLY

GLUTEN-FREE

LOW CALORIE

If it isn't already, fennel may well become one of the spices you cannot live without in your kitchen. It infuses this creamy soup with the gentle flavor of anise. If you don't have a spice grinder, use a mortar and pestle to grind the seed.

1 teaspoon freshly ground fennel seed

1 fennel bulb, cored and chopped

1 leek, white and pale green parts only, sliced thin

1 white potato, peeled and diced

⅛ teaspoon sea salt

2 cups low-sodium chicken broth

1 teaspoon white wine vinegar or lemon juice

2 tablespoons heavy cream

1 sprig fresh tarragon, roughly chopped (optional)

PREP
10 minutes

COOK
8 hours

PER SERVING
Calories: 200
Saturated Fat: 4g
Trans Fat: 0g
Carbohydrates: 32g
Fiber: 7g
Sodium: 269mg
Protein: 7g

1. Put the fennel seed, fennel bulb, leek, potato, salt, and broth in the slow cooker and stir to combine. Cover and cook on low for 8 hours.

2. Just before serving, add the vinegar to the crock and then purée the soup with an immersion blender. Stir in the heavy cream.

3. Serve garnished with fresh tarragon (if using).

VARIATION TIP To bring out even more flavor from the fennel seed, toast it in a dry skillet over medium heat for one to two minutes or until fragrant, then grind in a spice grinder.

SUBSTITUTION TIP To ensure the soup is Gluten-Free, use gluten-free low-sodium chicken broth.

HEART
HEALTHY

DIABETES
FRIENDLY

ALLERGY
FRIENDLY

GLUTEN-
FREE

LOW
CALORIE

PREP
10 minutes

COOK
8 hours

PER SERVING
Calories: 496
Saturated Fat: 1g
Trans Fat: 0g
Carbohydrates: 79g
Fiber: 33g
Sodium: 333mg
Protein: 33g

Sweet Spiced Lentil Soup

Serves 2

This recipe is brimming with holiday flavors and will make your house smell amazing. Traditionally, lentil soup is made with diced carrots, but apples make a surprising and delightful addition.

1 cup dried lentils, rinsed and sorted

1 apple, cored, peeled, and diced

1 cup diced onion

¼ cup diced celery

1 teaspoon fresh thyme

¼ teaspoon ground cinnamon

¼ teaspoon ground allspice

⅛ teaspoon sea salt

¼ cup dry red wine

3 cups low-sodium chicken or vegetable broth

1. Put all the ingredients into the slow cooker and stir to combine.

2. Cover and cook on low for 6 to 8 hours, until the lentils are very soft.

COOKING TIP You should always rinse and sort dried legumes. Sometimes you will find small rocks or sticks among them.

SUBSTITUTION TIP To ensure the soup is Allergy Friendly and Gluten-Free, use gluten-free low-sodium chicken or vegetable broth.

Split Pea Soup

Serves 2

HEART
HEALTHY

DIABETES
FRIENDLY

ALLERGY
FRIENDLY

GLUTEN-
FREE

LOW
CALORIE

The smoky flavor of the ham permeates this hearty, filling soup. If you would prefer a vegan version, use vegetable broth, and season with smoked sea salt or smoked paprika to impart a smoky flavor in the soup. This soup becomes a light meal when served with Simple Salad (page 134) and Whole-Grain Dinner Rolls (page 145).

1 cup dried green split peas, rinsed

¼ cup diced ham

¼ cup diced carrots

¼ cup diced onion

¼ cup diced celery

1 garlic clove, minced

3 cups low-sodium chicken broth

1 sprig fresh thyme

⅛ teaspoon sea salt

1. Put all the ingredients to the slow cooker and stir to combine.

2. Cover and cook on low for 8 to 10 hours. Remove the thyme sprig before serving.

NUTRITION TIP Dried peas are rich in protein and fiber and a good source of many vitamins and minerals, including manganese, copper, and B vitamins.

SUBSTITUTION TIP To ensure the soup is Allergy Friendly and Gluten-Free, use gluten-free low-sodium chicken broth.

PREP
5 minutes

COOK
8 to 10 hours

PER SERVING
Calories: 387
Saturated Fat: 1g
Trans Fat: 0g
Carbohydrates: 64g
Fiber: 26g
Sodium: 567mg
Protein: 35g

HEART
HEALTHY

DIABETES
FRIENDLY

LOW
CALORIE

PREP
10 minutes

COOK
8 hours

PER SERVING
Calories: 339
Saturated Fat: 4g
Trans Fat: 0g
Carbohydrates: 63g
Fiber: 15g
Sodium: 330mg
Protein: 8g

Rosemary Parsnip Bisque with Toasted Bread Crumbs

Serves 2

Rosemary lends its woodsy aroma to this sweet, creamy soup. It's delicious served with Fluffy Buttermilk Biscuits (page 146).

4 parsnips, peeled and cut into large chunks

½ cup diced onion

¼ cup diced celery

1 garlic clove, smashed

2 teaspoons fresh rosemary, divided

2 cups low-sodium chicken broth

⅛ teaspoon sea salt

2 tablespoons heavy cream

Freshly ground black pepper

¼ cup panko bread crumbs

1. Put the parsnips, onion, celery, garlic, and 1 teaspoon of rosemary in the slow cooker. Add the broth and salt and stir to combine.

2. Cover and cook on low for 8 hours.

3. Stir in the heavy cream and purée the soup with an immersion blender.

4. In a small bowl, mix together the remaining 1 teaspoon of rosemary, a few grinds of the black pepper, and the bread crumbs. Sprinkle some of this mixture over each serving of the soup.

SUBSTITUTION TIP If you want to make this a gluten-free soup, replace the panko with gluten-free bread crumbs, and be sure to use gluten-free low-sodium chicken broth.

Corn & Red Pepper Chowder

Serves 2

You can purchase roasted red peppers in a jar, or to make them yourself, halve, core, and seed the pepper and set it skin-side up on a broiler pan. Brush the pepper skin with a little extra-virgin olive oil and put the pan under a hot broiler. Once the pepper skin has charred, remove it from the broiler and transfer the pepper to a covered container to steam. Once it has cooled slightly, remove the skins and enjoy.

½ cup diced onion

1 cup diced roasted red bell pepper

2 Yukon Gold potatoes, peeled and diced

2 cups frozen corn kernels, thawed, divided

2 cups low-sodium chicken broth

1 teaspoon smoked paprika

½ teaspoon ground cumin

½ teaspoon ground coriander

⅛ teaspoon sea salt

Freshly ground black pepper

1 teaspoon red wine vinegar

2 tablespoons heavy cream (optional)

¼ cup thinly sliced scallions, white and green parts

1. Combine the onion, bell pepper, potatoes, 1 cup of corn kernels, broth, paprika, cumin, coriander, salt, and a few grinds of black pepper in the slow cooker and stir to combine.

2. Cover and cook on low for 8 hours.

3. Add the vinegar and heavy cream (if using) and purée the soup with an immersion blender. Stir in the remaining 1 cup of corn kernels and the scallions just before serving.

COOKING TIP For extra smokiness, use roasted corn kernels, which are also available frozen.

SUBSTITUTION TIP To ensure the soup is Gluten-Free, use gluten-free low-sodium chicken broth, and omit the cream to make it Allergy Friendly.

HEART HEALTHY

DIABETES FRIENDLY

ALLERGY FRIENDLY

GLUTEN-FREE

LOW CALORIE

PREP
10 minutes

COOK
8 hours

PER SERVING
Calories: 354
Saturated Fat: 4g
Trans Fat: 0g
Carbohydrates: 69g
Fiber: 8g
Sodium: 246mg
Protein: 11g

SOUPS & STEWS

HEART
HEALTHY

DIABETES
FRIENDLY

GLUTEN-
FREE

LOW
CALORIE

PREP
10 minutes

COOK
8 hours

PER SERVING
Calories: 175
Saturated Fat: 0g
Trans Fat: 0g
Carbohydrates: 30g
Fiber: 4g
Sodium: 196mg
Protein: 5g

Rutabaga & Sweet Potato Soup with Garlicky Ground Walnuts

Serves 2

Rutabaga is a root vegetable, also known as swede or yellow turnip. But don't mistake a rutabaga for an ordinary turnip! Rutabaga is a popular vegetable in Northern European countries, especially Finland, Norway, and Sweden. This savory soup is perfect on cold winter evenings and has a garlicky walnut pesto on top for contrast of flavor and texture.

2 cups peeled, diced rutabaga

1 cup peeled, diced sweet potato

1 leek, white and pale green parts only, sliced thin

⅛ teaspoon sea salt

2 cups low-sodium vegetable broth

1 sprig fresh sage, plus 1 teaspoon minced fresh sage

1 teaspoon minced garlic

2 tablespoons toasted walnuts

1. Put the rutabaga, sweet potato, leek, salt, broth, and sprig of sage into the slow cooker.

2. Cover and cook on low for 8 hours. Remove the sage sprig.

3. Use an immersion blender to purée the soup until smooth.

4. Place the 1 teaspoon minced fresh sage, garlic, and walnuts into a mortar and pestle and grind them into a paste. Serve each bowl of soup garnished with the walnut mixture.

COOKING TIP Toast the walnuts in a dry skillet over medium heat for one to two minutes or until fragrant.

SUBSTITUTION TIP To ensure this dish is Gluten-Free, use gluten-free low-sodium vegetable broth.

Baked Potato Soup

Serves 2

HEART
HEALTHY

DIABETES
FRIENDLY

GLUTEN-
FREE

LOW
CALORIE

Baked potatoes loaded with toppings can be a comforting, economical way to feed a growing family. This soup is a riff on the classic dinner, but without the chicken bouillon and ranch dressing mix often added to baked potato soups. It's still loaded with flavor, just not with calories.

2 russet potatoes, peeled and diced

½ cup minced onion

¼ cup minced celery

2 cups low-sodium chicken broth

⅛ teaspoon sea salt

1 tablespoon heavy cream

¼ cup thinly sliced scallions, white and green parts, for garnish

¼ cup grated sharp Cheddar cheese, for garnish

2 tablespoons crumbled cooked bacon, for garnish

PREP
10 minutes

COOK
8 hours

PER SERVING
Calories: 314
Saturated Fat: 6g
Trans Fat: 0g
Carbohydrates: 39g
Fiber: 6g
Sodium: 523mg
Protein: 13g

1. Put the potatoes, onion, celery, broth, and salt in the slow cooker, and stir together.

2. Cover and cook on low for 8 hours.

3. Stir in the cream and purée the soup with an immersion blender for a smooth soup. Or leave the soup chunky.

4. Serve garnished with the scallions, Cheddar cheese, and bacon.

NUTRITION TIP With their high glycemic index, potatoes are often looked down on. However, their impact on blood sugar levels is lowered by the presence of fat and protein in this dish.

SUBSTITUTION TIP To ensure the soup is Gluten-Free, use gluten-free low-sodium chicken broth.

HEART
HEALTHY

DIABETES
FRIENDLY

ALLERGY
FRIENDLY

GLUTEN-
FREE

LOW
CALORIE

PREP
10 minutes

COOK
8 hours

PER SERVING
Calories: 320
Saturated Fat: 1g
Trans Fat: 0g
Carbohydrates: 54g
Fiber: 22g
Sodium: 297mg
Protein: 9g

Minestrone

Serves 2

Minestrone soup is full of ingredients that form the basis of the Mediterranean diet—vegetables, beans, and extra-virgin olive oil. This soup pairs well with Whole-Grain Dinner Rolls (page 145).

2½ cups low-sodium vegetable broth

1 (15-ounce) can white beans, drained and rinsed

1 (15-ounce) can diced tomatoes, drained

½ cup diced red skin potatoes, skin on

½ cup diced celery

½ cup diced onion

½ cup diced carrots

¼ cup sliced mushrooms

¼ cup diced zucchini

¼ cup white rice

1 tablespoon minced garlic

1 tablespoon dried Italian seasoning

⅛ teaspoon sea salt

1 cup shredded kale

1 tablespoon extra-virgin olive oil, for garnish

1. Put the vegetable stock, beans, tomatoes, potatoes, celery, onion, carrots, mushrooms, zucchini, rice, garlic, Italian seasoning, and salt into the slow cooker and stir to combine.

2. Cover and cook on low for 6 to 8 hours.

3. Stir in the kale and let the soup sit until the kale is wilted, about 10 minutes.

4. Garnish each serving with a drizzle of the olive oil just before serving.

COOKING TIP Add even more flavor by selecting canned tomatoes that also include herbs and garlic.

SUBSTITUTION TIP To ensure the soup is Allergy Friendly and Gluten-Free, use gluten-free low-sodium vegetable broth. For added fiber, substitute the white rice with brown rice.

Chipotle Black Bean Soup

Serves 2

HEART HEALTHY

DIABETES FRIENDLY

ALLERGY FRIENDLY

GLUTEN-FREE

LOW CALORIE

PREP
10 minutes

COOK
8 hours

PER SERVING
Calories: 472
Saturated Fat: 4g
Trans Fat: 0g
Carbohydrates: 52g
Fiber: 20g
Sodium: 235mg
Protein: 19g

Chipotle peppers are large, smoke-dried jalapeño peppers. They have a mild heat but pack a delightful punch of smoky flavor. The peppers are available whole, dried, or packed in adobo sauce. The sauce, however, often contains wheat and other additives you may wish to avoid. Either may be used measure for measure in this recipe.

2 cups canned black beans, drained but not rinsed

1 teaspoon smoked paprika

1 teaspoon ground cumin

1 teaspoon ground coriander

1 teaspoon ground chipotle pepper

1 tablespoon tomato paste

½ cup diced onion

1 tablespoon minced garlic

⅛ teaspoon sea salt

2 cups low-sodium chicken or vegetable broth

Juice of ½ lime

1 small avocado, diced, for garnish

1. Put the black beans, paprika, cumin, coriander, chipotle chili, tomato paste, onion, garlic, salt, and broth into the slow cooker and stir to combine.

2. Cover and cook on low for 6 to 8 hours, until some of the beans are broken down but others still retain their shape.

3. Just before serving, stir in the lime juice. Garnish each serving with the avocado slices.

VARIATION TIP For even more flavor, toast the spices in a dry skillet over medium heat for 1 to 2 minutes or until fragrant before adding them to the crock.

SUBSTITUTION TIP To ensure the soup is Allergy Friendly and Gluten-Free, use gluten-free low-sodium chicken or vegetable broth.

HEART
HEALTHY

DIABETES
FRIENDLY

ALLERGY
FRIENDLY

GLUTEN-
FREE

LOW
CALORIE

PREP
10 minutes

COOK
8 hours

PER SERVING
Calories: 265
Saturated Fat: 13g
Trans Fat: 0g
Carbohydrates: 28g
Fiber: 5g
Sodium: 431mg
Protein: 8g

Red Curry Butternut Squash Soup

Serves 2

If you're not familiar with Thai red curry paste, you're in for a treat. It is a time-saving and economical way to imbue your food with traditional Thai flavors—red chili pepper, lemongrass, galangal root, and Kaffir lime—without having to scour a specialty market. The aromas of this soup are tantalizing.

2 cups cubed butternut squash

½ cup diced onion

1 teaspoon minced garlic

1 teaspoon minced ginger

2 cups low-sodium chicken broth

1 teaspoon Thai red curry paste

1 teaspoon fish sauce

½ cup coconut milk

1 teaspoon freshly squeezed lime juice

¼ cup fresh cilantro, for garnish

1. Put the butternut squash, onion, garlic, ginger, broth, curry paste, fish sauce, and coconut milk in the slow cooker. Stir gently to combine.

2. Cover and cook on low for 8 hours.

3. Just before serving, stir in the lime juice and garnish the soup with the cilantro.

NUTRITION TIP Coconut is naturally high in saturated fat, but it has been shown to aid in weight loss and improve energy levels. If you want a reduced-fat version of this soup, use light coconut milk or reduce the amount of coconut milk.

SUBSTITUTION TIP To ensure this soup is Allergy Friendly and Gluten-Free, use gluten-free low-sodium chicken broth. Many people also have allergies to fish sauce—you may substitute tamari if so.

Corn & Potato Chowder

Serves 2

Yukon Gold potatoes have a slightly sweet flavor and creamy texture that makes for a thick and luxurious soup. For even more creaminess, stir in just a few tablespoons of heavy cream. This recipe calls for frozen corn, but if you're making it in the summer, definitely use fresh corn.

2 cups frozen corn kernels, thawed, divided

½ cup diced onion

1 garlic clove, minced

3 Yukon Gold potatoes, peeled and diced

2 cups low-sodium chicken broth

1 thyme sprig

⅛ teaspoon sea salt

2 tablespoons heavy cream (optional)

1 scallion, white and green parts, sliced thin, for garnish

1. Put 1½ cups of corn kernels, the onion, garlic, potatoes, broth, thyme, and salt in the slow cooker and stir together. Cover and cook on low for 6 hours.

2. Remove the thyme sprig and add the heavy cream (if using) to the crock. Purée the soup with an immersion blender until it is smooth.

3. Garnish each serving with the remaining ½ cup of corn kernels and the scallions.

SUBSTITUTION TIP To ensure the soup is Gluten-Free, use gluten-free low-sodium chicken broth, and to make it Allergy Friendly, use coconut milk in place of the heavy cream or, if you're allergic to coconut, omit the cream altogether.

PREP
10 minutes

COOK
6 hours

PER SERVING
Calories: 409
Saturated Fat: 4g
Trans Fat: 0g
Carbohydrates: 82g
Fiber: 8g
Sodium: 223mg
Protein: 12g

HEART
HEALTHY

DIABETES
FRIENDLY

ALLERGY
FRIENDLY

GLUTEN-
FREE

LOW
CALORIE

PREP
15 minutes

COOK
6 to 8 hours

PER SERVING
Calories: 432
Saturated Fat: 26g
Trans Fat: 0g
Carbohydrates: 34g
Fiber: 14g
Sodium: 668mg
Protein: 9g

Vegetable Curry Soup

Serves 2

It's easy to overlook vegetables as nothing more than a side dish to the main course. Vegetables, however, are loaded with flavor and nutrients, and can be just as hearty and filling as meat. In this soup, they take center stage and bring a complexity of flavor and texture to the soup. Choose the shorter cooking time to help the vegetables retain their shape.

1 small eggplant, cut into 1-inch cubes, about 2 cups

1 teaspoon sea salt

1 cup quartered button mushrooms

1 onion, halved and sliced in thick half-circles

1 red bell pepper, cut into long strips

1 cup coconut milk

2 cups low-sodium chicken broth

1 tablespoon Thai red curry paste

1 tablespoon freshly squeezed lime juice

¼ cup fresh cilantro, for garnish

1. Put the eggplant in a colander over the sink. Sprinkle it with the salt and allow it to rest for 10 minutes, or up to 30 minutes if you have the time.

2. Put the mushrooms, onion, red bell pepper, coconut milk, broth, and red curry paste into the slow cooker.

3. Rinse the eggplant in the colander and gently press to squeeze out any excess moisture from each cube. Add the eggplant to the slow cooker. Stir the ingredients to combine.

4. Cover and cook on low for 6 to 8 hours.

5. Just before serving, stir in the lime juice and garnish each serving with the cilantro.

VARIATION TIP To increase the protein in this recipe, add one boneless, skinless chicken breast to the soup at the beginning of the cooking time. When the soup is ready, remove the breast and dice it, returning the pieces to the soup. To increase the carbohydrates, add 2 ounces of rice noodles to the soup about 10 minutes before serving.

SUBSTITUTION TIP To make sure the soup is Allergy Friendly and Gluten-Free, use gluten-free low-sodium chicken broth.

Pumpkin Black Bean Chili

Serves 2

Pumpkin and chili are two fall favorites that marry beautifully in this thick vegetarian stew. You can use other types of beans, such as pinto or kidney beans, if you wish. Consider serving the chili with a big slice of Corn Bread (page 147).

1 cup canned black beans, drained and rinsed

1 cup canned fire-roasted diced tomatoes, drained

1 cup unsweetened pumpkin purée

½ cup diced onion

½ cup diced green bell pepper

1 teaspoon minced garlic

1 teaspoon ground Ancho chile

1 teaspoon smoked paprika

⅛ teaspoon cinnamon

⅛ teaspoon sea salt

¼ cup shredded Cheddar cheese, for garnish

2 tablespoons sour cream, for garnish

¼ cup roughly chopped fresh cilantro, for garnish

1. Put the beans, tomatoes, pumpkin, onion, bell pepper, garlic, chili powder, paprika, cinnamon, and salt in the slow cooker, and stir to combine.

2. Cover and cook on low for 8 hours.

3. Garnish each serving with the Cheddar cheese, sour cream, and fresh cilantro.

NUTRITION TIP Pumpkin purée needn't be reserved for Thanksgiving pies. It's loaded with nutrients, especially vitamin A; just 1 cup has nearly 200 percent of your daily requirement.

HEART HEALTHY

DIABETES FRIENDLY

GLUTEN-FREE

LOW CALORIE

PREP
10 minutes

COOK
8 hours

PER SERVING
Calories: 301
Saturated Fat: 5g
Trans Fat: 0g
Carbohydrates: 43g
Fiber: 14g
Sodium: 426mg
Protein: 15g

HEART
HEALTHY

DIABETES
FRIENDLY

LOW
CALORIE

PREP
10 minutes

COOK
8 hours

PER SERVING
Calories: 320
Saturated Fat: 2g
Trans Fat: 0g
Carbohydrates: 24g
Fiber: 3g
Sodium: 354mg
Protein: 34g

Chicken Noodle Soup

Serves 2

The bone helps keep the chicken moist during the long, slow cooking and imbues the broth with body and rich flavor. But, if you prefer the convenience, use a large boneless, skinless chicken breast instead. The aroma of this soup is warm and welcoming after a long day of work.

1 bone-in chicken breast, skin removed, about 8 to 12 ounces

1 cup diced carrots

1 cup diced celery

3 garlic cloves, minced

1 sprig fresh thyme

2 cups low-sodium chicken broth

⅛ teaspoon sea salt

4 ounces egg noodles

1 teaspoon red wine vinegar

Freshly ground black pepper

1. Put the chicken, carrots, celery, garlic, thyme, broth, and salt in the slow cooker and stir to combine.

2. Cover and cook on low for 8 hours.

3. Remove the thyme and discard it. Remove the chicken to a cutting board and shred it with a fork. Discard the bone.

4. Add the egg noodles to the slow cooker, cover the crock, and cook until the noodles are tender, about 10 minutes. Return the shredded chicken to the crock and stir in the vinegar. Season with the black pepper.

SUBSTITUTION TIP For an Allergy Friendly and Gluten-Free soup, choose gluten-free chicken broth and noodles, or simply omit the noodles for a low-carbohydrate version.

Garlicky Chicken Kale Soup

Serves 2

HEART
HEALTHY

DIABETES
FRIENDLY

ALLERGY
FRIENDLY

GLUTEN-
FREE

LOW
CALORIE

The garlic and red pepper flakes liven up the kale and the tender meat in this flavorful soup. You may be accustomed to cooking with the leaner white meat of the chicken, but the thighs add a negligible amount of fat and calories to the dish and a lot more flavor. This soup is wonderful with Whole-Grain Dinner Rolls (page 145).

2 boneless, skinless chicken thighs, diced

1 small onion, halved and sliced thin

2 carrots, peeled and diced

6 garlic cloves, roughly chopped

2 cups low-sodium chicken broth

⅛ teaspoon sea salt

⅛ teaspoon red pepper flakes

Zest of 1 lemon

Juice of 1 lemon

2 cups shredded fresh kale

PREP
10 minutes

COOK
6 hours

1. Put the chicken, onion, carrots, garlic, broth, salt, red pepper flakes, and lemon zest in the slow cooker and stir to combine.

2. Cover and cook on low for 6 hours.

3. Stir in the lemon juice and kale just before serving.

PER SERVING
Calories: 361
Saturated Fat: 3g
Trans Fat: 0g
Carbohydrates: 20g
Fiber: 3g
Sodium: 354mg
Protein: 45g

NUTRITION TIP Adding the kale at the last minute helps it retain its nutrients, many of which would otherwise be lost during the long cooking time.

SUBSTITUTION TIP To ensure this soup is Allergy Friendly and Gluten-Free, use gluten-free low-sodium chicken broth.

HEART
HEALTHY

DIABETES
FRIENDLY

GLUTEN-
FREE

PREP
10 minutes

COOK
8 hours

PER SERVING
Calories: 498
Saturated Fat: 6g
Trans Fat: 0g
Carbohydrates: 47g
Fiber: 9g
Sodium: 435mg
Protein: 34g

Chicken Fajita Soup

Serves 2

This spicy soup tastes even better with a handful of crunchy tortilla chips and a touch of sour cream, which is why they are included in the ingredient list. If you prefer a milder soup, reduce the red pepper flakes to just a pinch. For a lower-calorie or dairy-free soup, omit the cheese.

2 bone-in, skinless chicken thighs

½ cup frozen corn, thawed

½ cup canned fire-roasted diced tomatoes

½ cup canned black beans, drained and rinsed

½ cup diced onions

¼ teaspoon red chili flakes

2 garlic cloves, minced

2 cups low-sodium chicken broth

1 tablespoon ground cumin

1 teaspoon smoked paprika

⅛ teaspoon sea salt

2 tablespoons shredded sharp Cheddar cheese

¼ cup minced fresh cilantro

1 tablespoon freshly squeezed lime juice

1 cup corn tortilla chips, for garnish

Sour cream, for garnish (optional)

1. Put the chicken, corn, tomatoes, beans, onions, red chili flakes, garlic, broth, cumin, and paprika in the slow cooker and stir to combine.

2. Cover and cook on low for 8 hours.

3. Remove the chicken to a cutting board. Stir the cheese into the soup. While the cheese melts, shred the chicken with a fork. Stir the meat back into the soup along with the cilantro and lime juice.

4. Serve the soup garnished with the tortilla chips and a dollop of sour cream.

SERVING TIP Always add fresh cilantro to recipes just before serving. Its flavor virtually disappears when cooked for more than a few minutes.

SUBSTITUTION TIP To ensure the soup is Gluten-Free, use gluten-free low-sodium chicken broth.

Beef Barley Soup

Serves 2

HEART
HEALTHY

DIABETES
FRIENDLY

LOW
CALORIE

PREP
10 minutes

COOK
8 hours

PER SERVING
Calories: 362
Saturated Fat: 3g
Trans Fat: 0g
Carbohydrates: 32g
Fiber: 7g
Sodium: 634mg
Protein: 40g

This hearty soup is perfect after a long day of outdoor winter activities. It has complex carbohydrates from the barley and satiating protein from the beef. The soup is savory and satisfying on its own or served with Whole-Grain Dinner Rolls (page 145).

8 ounces beef stew meat, trimmed of fat and cut into 1-inch cubes

¼ cup pearl barley

1 cup diced onion

1 cup diced carrot

1 teaspoon fresh thyme

½ teaspoon dried oregano

2 cups low-sodium beef stock

⅛ teaspoon sea salt

1. Put all the ingredients in the slow cooker and stir to combine.

2. Cover and cook on low for 8 hours. The meat should be tender and the barley soft.

VARIATION TIP Have additional vegetable scraps lying around? Pretty much any mild-flavored vegetable or herb will work well in this soup. Consider adding parsnips, potatoes, green beans, mushrooms, rosemary, or parsley.

HEART
HEALTHY

ALLERGY
FRIENDLY

GLUTEN-
FREE

LOW
CALORIE

PREP
10 minutes

COOK
6 to 8 hours

PER SERVING
Calories: 599
Saturated Fat: 3g
Trans Fat: 0g
Carbohydrates: 91g
Fiber: 22g
Sodium: 534mg
Protein: 35g

Lentil, Chickpea & White Bean Stew

Serves 2

This hearty stew is rich in complex carbohydrates for sustained energy. It's perfect after a long day of skiing or hiking in the winter. The legumes can be replaced with alternative varieties, but do not use dry beans in the slow cooker. They will not cook quickly enough to ensure food safety.

½ cup canned chickpeas, drained and rinsed

½ cup canned white beans, drained and rinsed

½ cup lentils, rinsed and sorted

½ cup white rice

½ cup diced carrots

½ cup diced red bell pepper

¼ cup parsley

1 ounce pancetta, diced

2 cups low-sodium vegetable broth

⅛ teaspoon sea salt

1. Put all the ingredients into the slow cooker and stir to mix thoroughly.

2. Cover and cook on low for 6 to 8 hours.

COOKING TIP To make this soup vegan, replace the pancetta with ½ teaspoon liquid smoke and 1 tablespoon olive oil.

SUBSTITUTION TIP To ensure the soup is Allergy Friendly and Gluten-Free, use gluten-free low-sodium vegetable broth.

Spicy Mediterranean Beef Stew with Pearl Barley

Serves 2

Beef simmered low and slow in wine is a classic around the globe. It seems that every culture has a way of transforming tough cuts of meat into an elegant meal. In Greece, beef is cooked in red wine and vinegar along with an array of spices for a tangy, spicy stew called *stifado*.

¼ cup dry pearl barley

½ cup water

½ teaspoon ground cinnamon

½ teaspoon ground coriander

Freshly ground black pepper

⅛ teaspoon sea salt

1 tablespoon tomato paste

¼ cup red wine vinegar

1 cup dry red wine

12 ounces beef brisket, cut into 1-inch cubes

½ cup minced onions

¼ cup minced celery

2 garlic cloves, minced

2 tablespoons minced fresh flat-leaf parsley

1. Put the pearl barley and water in the slow cooker and give it a stir to make sure all the barley is submerged.

2. In a large bowl, combine the cinnamon, coriander, a few grinds of the black pepper, salt, tomato paste, vinegar, and red wine. Add the beef, onions, celery, garlic, and parsley to the bowl and stir together. Gently pour this mixture over the barley. Do not stir.

3. Cover and cook on low for 8 hours.

SUBSTITUTION TIP To make this dish Allergy Friendly or Gluten-Free, use wild rice instead of the pearl barley.

HEART HEALTHY

DIABETES FRIENDLY

LOW CALORIE

PREP
10 minutes

COOK
8 hours

PER SERVING
Calories: 536
Saturated Fat: 4g
Trans Fat: 0g
Carbohydrates: 29g
Fiber: 6g
Sodium: 262mg
Protein: 55g

four
Vegetarian & Vegan Dishes

62 Barbecue
Kabocha Squash

63 Braised Quinoa,
Kale & Summer Squash

64 Rosemary
Cauliflower & Lentils

65 Mixed Bean Chili

66 Curried Sweet Potatoes
with Broccoli & Cashews

67 Moroccan-Style Chickpeas
with Chard

68 Spinach & Black Bean
Enchilada Pie

69 Spinach, Mushroom &
Swiss Cheese Crustless Quiche

70 Seitan Tikka Masala

71 Butter Seitan & Chickpeas

72 Tempeh Shepherd's Pie

73 Tempeh-Stuffed
Bell Peppers

74 Tofu Red Curry with
Green Beans

75 Tofu Stir-Fry

76 Spicy Peanut Rice Bake

77 Vegetarian Cassoulet

ALLERGY
FRIENDLY

GLUTEN-
FREE

LOW
CALORIE

PREP
10 minutes

COOK
6 to 8 hours

PER SERVING
Calories: 236
Saturated Fat: 0g
Trans Fat: 0g
Carbohydrates: 48g
Fiber: 11g
Sodium: 839mg
Protein: 7g

Barbecue
Kabocha Squash

Serves 2

I fell in love with kabocha squash after my friend Anna served it roasted it in the oven with red onions and sweet potatoes. Those same ingredients are combined in this recipe along with the tangy spices of a good barbecue sauce. This dish goes well over Cilantro Rice Pilaf (page 140) or with Fluffy Buttermilk Biscuits (page 146).

1 teaspoon extra-virgin olive oil

½ kabocha squash, seeded, peeled, and cut into 2-by-1-inch pieces

1 red onion, halved and sliced thin

1 small sweet potato, cut into 1-inch pieces

1 cup tomato sauce

½ cup low-sodium vegetable broth

1 teaspoon Dijon mustard

1 teaspoon smoked paprika

1 teaspoon garlic powder

1 teaspoon onion powder

1 teaspoon maple syrup or honey

⅛ teaspoon sea salt

1. Grease the inside of the slow cooker with the olive oil.

2. Put the squash, red onion, and sweet potato into the slow cooker.

3. In a small bowl, whisk together the tomato sauce, vegetable broth, mustard, paprika, garlic powder, onion powder, maple syrup, and salt. Pour this mixture over the vegetables.

4. Cover and cook on low for 6 to 8 hours, or until the squash is very tender.

COOKING TIP Kabocha squash has an intimidating appearance, but with a sharp knife and a little bit of confidence, it's easy to cut and peel. First, cut the squash in half vertically. Remove the seeds with a spoon and then slice each half into four wedges, for a total of eight wedges. Use a paring knife or vegetable peeler to remove the tough green peel from each wedge.

SUBSTITUTION TIP To ensure this recipe is Allergy Friendly and Gluten-Free, use gluten-free low-sodium vegetable broth.

Braised Quinoa, Kale & Summer Squash

Serves 2

This vegetarian dish is rich in fiber, vitamins, and minerals. Note the short cooking time; the texture of the squash will become soft and mushy if cooked longer, though it is fine to do so. Consider serving it with Whole-Grain Dinner Rolls (page 145) or Simple Salad (page 134).

½ cup quinoa

½ cup canned chickpeas, drained and rinsed

1 cup diced summer squash

4 cups fresh kale

1 cup canned plum tomatoes, roughly chopped

2 cups low-sodium vegetable broth

1 tablespoon Italian herb blend

⅛ teaspoon sea salt

PREP
10 minutes

COOK
4 hours

PER SERVING
Calories: 342
Saturated Fat: 1g
Trans Fat: 0g
Carbohydrates: 56g
Fiber: 8g
Sodium: 456mg
Protein: 19g

1. Put all the ingredients into the slow cooker, stirring to mix them together thoroughly.

2. Cover and cook on low for 4 hours.

VARIATION TIP Consider swapping the kale for another leafy green, such as chard or collard greens.

SUBSTITUTION TIP To ensure the soup is Allergy Friendly and Gluten-Free, use gluten-free low-sodium vegetable broth.

HEART
HEALTHY

DIABETES
FRIENDLY

ALLERGY
FRIENDLY

GLUTEN-
FREE

LOW
CALORIE

PREP
10 minutes

COOK
8 hours

PER SERVING
Calories: 484
Saturated Fat: 2g
Trans Fat: 0g
Carbohydrates: 65g
Fiber: 32g
Sodium: 189mg
Protein: 34g

Rosemary Cauliflower & Lentils

Serves 2

The flavor of fresh rosemary holds up beautifully during long, slow cooking. Its earthiness is offset by the brightness of lemon and subtle sweetness of roasted garlic for a flavorful and satisfying vegan dinner.

1 cup cauliflower florets

1 cup lentils

1 tablespoon fresh rosemary

1 tablespoon roasted garlic

Zest of 1 lemon

1 tablespoon extra-virgin olive oil

⅛ teaspoon sea salt

Freshly ground black pepper

3 cups low-sodium vegetable broth

Juice of 1 lemon

¼ cup roughly chopped fresh parsley

1. Put the cauliflower, lentils, rosemary, garlic, lemon zest, and olive oil in the slow cooker. Season with the salt and black pepper.

2. Pour the vegetable broth over the cauliflower and lentils. Cover and cook on low for 8 hours.

3. Just before serving, drizzle the cauliflower and lentils with the lemon juice and sprinkle the parsley over the top.

NUTRITION TIP High-fiber foods such as lentils have been shown to help lower blood cholesterol and may reduce your risk for heart disease.

SUBSTITUTION TIP To ensure this recipe is Allergy Friendly and Gluten-Free, use gluten-free low-sodium vegetable broth.

Mixed Bean Chili

Serves 2

ALLERGY
FRIENDLY

GLUTEN-
FREE

LOW
CALORIE

PREP
10 minutes

COOK
6 to 8 hours

PER SERVING
Calories: 257
Saturated Fat: 0g
Trans Fat: 0g
Carbohydrates: 58g
Fiber: 17g
Sodium: 1067mg
Protein: 13g

The variety of flavors and textures of mixed beans gives this chili a filling, stick-to-your-ribs quality. If you cannot find a can of mixed beans, purchase two or three cans of individual types of beans, such as kidney beans, black beans, and pinto beans. Drain and rinse the beans; leftover beans can be stored in the refrigerator for up to two days or in a sealed container in the freezer for several weeks.

1 (16-ounce) can mixed beans, drained and rinsed

1 cup frozen roasted corn kernels, thawed

1 cup canned fire-roasted diced tomatoes, undrained

½ cup diced onion

2 garlic cloves, minced

1 teaspoon ground cumin

1 teaspoon smoked paprika

1 teaspoon dried oregano

⅛ teaspoon sea salt

1. Put all the ingredients in the slow cooker. Give them a quick stir to combine.

2. Cover and cook on low for 6 to 8 hours.

COOKING TIP Some beans are sturdier than others. Soft beans such as cannellini break down quickly while firm beans such as kidneys withstand the longer cooking time. If you want the beans to retain their shape, choose the shorter cooking time.

HEART
HEALTHY

DIABETES
FRIENDLY

GLUTEN-
FREE

LOW
CALORIE

PREP
10 minutes

COOK
6 to 8 hours

PER SERVING
Calories: 582
Saturated Fat: 27g
Trans Fat: 0g
Carbohydrates: 60g
Fiber: 12g
Sodium: 53mg
Protein: 10g

Curried Sweet Potatoes with Broccoli & Cashews

Serves 2

Sweet potatoes are a wonderful source of complex carbohydrates, vitamins, and minerals, especially vitamin A. Paired with broccoli, coconut milk, and cashews, they provide a filling and delicious vegan dinner.

2 medium sweet potatoes, cut into 1-inch pieces

1 cup broccoli florets

½ cup diced onions

1 cup light coconut milk

1 teaspoon minced fresh ginger

1 teaspoon minced garlic

Pinch red pepper flakes

1 tablespoon curry powder

1 teaspoon garam masala

¼ cup toasted cashews

1. Put the sweet potatoes, broccoli, and onions into the slow cooker.

2. In a small bowl, whisk together the coconut milk, ginger, garlic, red pepper flakes, curry powder, and garam masala. Pour this mixture over the vegetables.

3. Cover and cook on low for 6 to 8 hours until the vegetables are very tender but not falling apart.

4. Just before serving, add the cashews and stir thoroughly.

COOKING TIP To extend their shelf life, store sweet potatoes in a cool, dark place away from onions and garlic, which hasten spoilage.

Moroccan-Style Chickpeas with Chard

Serves 2

The fragrant spices in this healthy vegan dish create a warm, enticing aroma. The Swiss chard cooks way down, so don't worry if it's challenging to fit everything into the slow cooker initially. Look for rainbow chard—its multicolored stems offer a great array of nutrients.

½ bunch Swiss chard, stems diced and leaves roughly chopped

1 (16-ounce) can chickpeas, drained and rinsed

½ cup diced onion

½ cup diced carrots

¼ cup diced dried apricots

2 tablespoons roughly chopped preserved lemons (optional)

1 tablespoon tomato paste

1 teaspoon minced fresh ginger

¼ teaspoon red pepper flakes

½ teaspoon smoked paprika

½ teaspoon ground cinnamon

¼ teaspoon ground cumin

⅛ teaspoon sea salt

1. Put all the ingredients into the slow cooker. Stir everything together thoroughly.

2. Cover and cook on low for 8 hours.

NUTRITION TIP Swiss chard is a rich source of micronutrients, rivaling spinach in its nutrient density. It is an especially good source of flavonoids, which are good for heart health.

PREP
10 minutes

COOK
8 hours

PER SERVING
Calories: 84
Saturated Fat: 0g
Trans Fat: 0g
Carbohydrates: 17g
Fiber: 5g
Sodium: 379mg
Protein: 4g

PREP
10 minutes

COOK
6 to 8 hours

PER SERVING
Calories: 373
Saturated Fat: 10g
Trans Fat: g
Carbohydrates: 42g
Fiber: 11g
Sodium: 234mg
Protein: 13g

Spinach & Black Bean Enchilada Pie

Serves 2

This savory vegetarian dish is one of my husband's favorites. He makes it just for himself sometimes when I'm going to be out for the evening. For added flavor, toast the cumin seeds in a dry skillet for a couple minutes, grind in a spice grinder or with a mortar and pestle just before adding them.

1 (15-ounce) can black beans, drained and rinsed

¼ cup low-fat cream cheese

¼ cup low-fat Cheddar cheese

½ cup minced onion

1 teaspoon minced garlic

1 teaspoon ground cumin

1 teaspoon smoked paprika

2 cups shredded fresh spinach

1 teaspoon extra-virgin olive oil

1 cup enchilada sauce, divided

4 corn tortillas

¼ cup fresh cilantro, for garnish

1. In a large bowl, mix together the beans, cream cheese, Cheddar cheese, onion, garlic, cumin, paprika, and spinach.

2. Grease the inside of the slow cooker with the olive oil.

3. Pour ¼ cup of enchilada sauce into the crock, spreading it across the bottom. Place one corn tortilla on top of the sauce. Top the tortilla with one-third of the black bean and spinach mixture. Top this with a second corn tortilla and then slather it with ¼ cup of enchilada sauce. Repeat this layering, finishing with a corn tortilla and the last ¼ cup of enchilada sauce.

4. Cover and cook on low for 6 to 8 hours. Garnish with the cilantro just before serving.

COOKING TIP Choose an imported enchilada sauce from the international foods section of the grocery store. Unlike other jarred enchilada sauces, it typically contains no added cream or fat.

Spinach, Mushroom & Swiss Cheese Crustless Quiche

Serves 2

PREP
10 minutes

COOK
8 hours

PER SERVING
Calories: 348
Saturated Fat: 9g
Trans Fat: 0g
Carbohydrates: 21g
Fiber: 6g
Sodium: 444mg
Protein: 24g

The ingredients in this quiche are rich in moisture. For a more intense flavor, before adding them to the slow cooker, sauté the mushrooms in butter on the stovetop for 5 to 10 minutes, then remove them from the pan. Add the spinach to the same skillet and wilt it just until the water evaporates, 1 to 2 minutes. You can also use frozen spinach by defrosting it first under running water and then squeezing out excess moisture.

1 teaspoon butter, at room temperature, or extra-virgin olive oil

4 eggs

1 teaspoon fresh thyme

⅛ teaspoon sea salt

Freshly ground black pepper

2 slices whole-grain bread, crusts removed, cut into 1-inch cubes

½ cup diced button mushrooms

2 tablespoons minced onion

1 cup shredded spinach

½ cup shredded Swiss cheese

1. Grease the inside of the slow cooker with the butter.

2. In a small bowl, whisk together the eggs, thyme, salt, and a few grinds of the black pepper.

3. Put the bread, mushrooms, onions, spinach, and cheese in the slow cooker. Pour the egg mixture over the top and stir gently to combine.

4. Cover and cook on low for 8 hours or overnight.

NUTRITION TIP Swiss cheese is naturally low in calories and rich in protein, with 8 grams per 1 ounce serving.

PREP
10 minutes

COOK
6 hours

PER SERVING
Calories: 245
Saturated Fat: 3g
Trans Fat: 0g
Carbohydrates: 24g
Fiber: 8g
Sodium: 733mg
Protein: 4g

Seitan Tikka Masala

Serves 2

Seitan (pronounced *say-tan*) has the most similar texture to chicken of any of the vegetarian proteins. It is made with vital wheat gluten, so it is decidedly not gluten-free. The long, slow cooking time allows it to absorb all the enticing flavors in this dish. Consider serving it with Cilantro Rice Pilaf (page 140).

8 ounces seitan, cut into bite-size pieces	1 teaspoon smoked paprika
1 cup chopped green beans	⅛ teaspoon red pepper flakes
1 cup diced onion	1 teaspoon minced fresh ginger
1 cup fire-roasted tomatoes, drained	1 cup low-sodium vegetable broth
1 teaspoon ground coriander	2 tablespoons coconut cream
1 teaspoon ground cumin	¼ cup minced fresh cilantro, for garnish

1. Put the seitan, green beans, onion, tomatoes, coriander, cumin, paprika, red pepper flakes, ginger, and vegetable broth in the slow cooker. Gently stir the ingredients together to combine.

2. Cover and cook on low for 6 hours.

3. Allow to the dish to rest, uncovered, for 10 minutes, then stir in the coconut cream and garnish the dish with the cilantro.

SUBSTITUTION TIP If you follow a gluten-free diet, you can use tempeh instead of seitan. It may crumble slightly, but the flavors will taste just as good, and be sure to use gluten-free low-sodium vegetable broth.

Butter Seitan & Chickpeas

Serves 2

PREP
10 minutes

COOK
6 to 8 hours

Who says chicken has to be the star? Seitan shines in this vegan version of a classic Indian recipe. It's a warm and comforting dish that even die-hard meat lovers will enjoy. This dish is especially nice with Cilantro Rice Pilaf (page 140).

1 teaspoon extra-virgin olive oil

8 ounces seitan, cut into bite-size pieces

1 (15-ounce) can chickpeas, drained and rinsed

½ cup minced onion

1 teaspoon minced garlic

2 tablespoons tomato paste

1 teaspoon minced fresh ginger

½ teaspoon garam masala

1 teaspoon curry powder

Pinch red pepper flakes

½ teaspoon sea salt

1 cup light coconut milk

PER SERVING
Calories: 302
Saturated Fat: 12g
Trans Fat: 0g
Carbohydrates: 17g
Fiber: 4g
Sodium: 995mg
Protein: 4g

1. Grease the inside of the slow cooker with the olive oil.

2. Put all the ingredients into the slow cooker and stir to mix thoroughly.

3. Cover and cook on low for 6 to 8 hours.

SUBSTITUTION TIP To further reduce the calories in this dish, cut the amount of coconut milk in half and use ½ cup low-sodium vegetable broth.

HEART
HEALTHY

DIABETES
FRIENDLY

GLUTEN-
FREE

LOW
CALORIE

PREP
10 minutes

COOK
8 hours

PER SERVING
Calories: 476
Saturated Fat: 6g
Trans Fat: 0g
Carbohydrates: 53g
Fiber: 8g
Sodium: 338mg
Protein: 32g

Tempeh Shepherd's Pie

Serves 2

I grew up on traditional shepherd's pie. It was the 1980s, and I'm pretty sure my mother rinsed the ground beef after she browned it to get rid of any trace of fat. Fortunately, tempeh naturally has 30 percent less fat than ground beef and 25 percent more protein, making this vegetarian shepherd's pie healthy comfort food at its finest. To make this recipe vegan, use a vegan cheese shred or omit the cheese altogether.

1 cup frozen peas, thawed

1 cup diced carrots

½ cup minced onions

8 ounces tempeh

⅛ teaspoon sea salt

Freshly ground black pepper

1½ cups prepared mashed potatoes

2 tablespoons shredded sharp Cheddar cheese

1. Put the peas, carrots, onions, and tempeh in the slow cooker and gently stir to combine. Season the mixture with the salt and black pepper.

2. Spread the prepared mashed potatoes over the tempeh and vegetable mixture.

3. Cover and cook on low for 8 hours.

4. Sprinkle with the cheese just before serving.

COOKING TIP This recipe is perfect for using up leftover mashed potatoes. Or, if you have instant potato flakes on hand, simply heat 1 cup water, 1 teaspoon butter, and ½ cup 2% milk in a small pot over medium heat until it comes to the barest simmer. Stir in 1 cup potato flakes and mix until just combined.

Tempeh-Stuffed Bell Peppers

Serves 2

HEART HEALTHY

DIABETES FRIENDLY

GLUTEN-FREE

LOW CALORIE

PREP
10 minutes

COOK
6 to 8 hours

PER SERVING
Calories: 422
Saturated Fat: 5g
Trans Fat: 0g
Carbohydrates: 44g
Fiber: 8g
Sodium: 184mg
Protein: 28g

Bell peppers and other "fillable" vegetables are a mainstay in my house. Between the four of us, we all have different dietary restrictions. Being able to customize each portion based each person's needs keeps dinner healthy and enjoyable for everyone.

1 teaspoon extra-virgin olive oil

8 ounces tempeh, crumbled

1 cup frozen corn kernels, thawed

¼ cup minced onions

1 teaspoon minced garlic

1 teaspoon ground cumin

1 teaspoon smoked paprika

2 tablespoons pepper Jack cheese

⅛ teaspoon sea salt

4 narrow red bell peppers

1. Grease the inside of the slow cooker with the olive oil.

2. In a medium bowl, combine the tempeh, corn, onions, garlic, cumin, paprika, cheese, and salt.

3. Cut the tops off each of the peppers and set the tops aside. Scoop out and discard the seeds and membranes from inside each pepper. Divide the tempeh filling among the peppers. Return the tops to each of the peppers.

4. Nestle the peppers into the slow cooker.

5. Cover and cook on low for 6 to 8 hours, until the peppers are very tender.

COOKING TIP Red, orange, and yellow bell peppers are sweeter than green bell peppers, but you could certainly use green if you prefer.

HEART
HEALTHY

DIABETES
FRIENDLY

GLUTEN-
FREE

LOW
CALORIE

PREP
10 minutes

COOK
6 hours

PER SERVING
Calories: 538
Saturated Fat: 28g
Trans Fat: 0g
Carbohydrates: 25g
Fiber: 10g
Sodium: 350mg
Protein: 25g

Tofu Red Curry with Green Beans

Serves 2

One of tofu's greatest selling points—other than being a great vegan source of protein—is that it is virtually tasteless, so you can impart whatever flavors you want to it with the other ingredients in the dish. The slow cooker makes this flavor infusion even more robust, giving the tofu hours to soak up the rich, spicy coconut curry broth. It is delicious served with Cilantro Rice Pilaf (page 140) or the Chilled Rice Noodle Salad (page 142).

1 teaspoon extra-virgin olive oil

16 ounces firm tofu, drained and cut into 1-inch pieces

2 cups chopped green beans

½ red onion, halved and sliced thin

1 plum tomato, diced

1 teaspoon minced fresh ginger

1 teaspoon minced garlic

2 teaspoons Thai red curry paste

1 cup coconut milk

1 cup low-sodium vegetable broth

1. Grease the inside of the slow cooker with the olive oil.

2. Put all the ingredients into the slow cooker, and stir gently.

3. Cover and cook on low for 6 hours.

NUTRITION TIP The fats in coconut milk are a good source of energy. If you're an athlete engaged in endurance activities, you may want to swap the coconut milk for coconut cream because it has a higher fat content.

SUBSTITUTION TIP To ensure this recipe is Gluten-Free, use gluten-free low-sodium vegetable broth.

Tofu Stir-Fry

GLUTEN-FREE

LOW CALORIE

PREP
10 minutes

COOK
4 to 6 hours

PER SERVING
Calories: 456
Saturated Fat: 3g
Trans Fat: 0g
Carbohydrates: 63g
Fiber: 9g
Sodium: 1230mg
Protein: 26g

When my husband and I were first married, we had a weekly grocery budget of $20. Tofu stir-fry was a standing item on our weekly menu because the ingredients were inexpensive, flavorful, easily available, and full of nutrition. Who says it costs a lot to eat healthy?

1 teaspoon extra-virgin olive oil

½ cup brown rice

1 cup water

Pinch sea salt

1 (16-ounce) block tofu, drained and cut into 1-inch pieces

1 green bell pepper, cored and cut into long strips

½ onion, halved and thinly sliced

1 cup chopped green beans, cut into 1-inch pieces

2 carrots, cut into ½-inch dice

2 tablespoons low-sodium soy sauce

1 tablespoon hoisin sauce

1 tablespoon freshly squeezed lime juice

1 teaspoon minced garlic

Pinch red pepper flakes

1. Grease the inside of the slow cooker with the olive oil.

2. Put the brown rice, water, and salt in the slow cooker and gently stir so all the rice grains are submerged.

3. Put the tofu, bell pepper, onion, green beans, and carrots over the rice.

4. In a measuring cup or glass jar, whisk together the soy sauce, hoisin sauce, lime juice, garlic, and red pepper flakes. Pour this mixture over the tofu and vegetables.

5. Cover and cook on low for 4 to 6 hours, until the rice has soaked up all the liquid and the vegetables are tender.

COOKING TIP Choose organic, non-GMO tofu to avoid ingesting herbicide residue. Genetically engineered soybean crops allow the plant to withstand the application of pesticide glyphosate (Roundup), which is now recognized as a probable carcinogen by the World Health Organization.

SUBSTITUTION TIP To ensure this recipe is Gluten-Free, use gluten-free soy sauce.

PREP
10 minutes

COOK
6 to 8 hours

PER SERVING
Calories: 554
Saturated Fat: 13g
Trans Fat: 0g
Carbohydrates: 59g
Fiber: 10g
Sodium: 401mg
Protein: 24g

Spicy Peanut Rice Bake

Serves 2

My husband has been a vegetarian for nearly 20 years, but had never tried African-style peanut soup until I made it for him while writing this book. This slow-cooker version isn't exactly authentic, but it sure is tasty!

1 teaspoon extra-virgin olive oil

½ cup brown rice

3 cups low-sodium vegetable broth, divided

4 collard leaves, ribs removed, chopped into thin ribbons

½ cup minced red onion

1 tablespoon minced ginger

2 tablespoons tomato paste

¼ cup unsalted creamy peanut butter

1 teaspoon Sriracha

⅛ teaspoon sea salt

¼ cup roughly chopped cilantro, for garnish

Lime wedges, for garnish

2 tablespoons roasted peanuts, roughly chopped, for garnish

1. Grease the inside of the slow cooker with olive oil.

2. Put the rice, 2 cups of broth, collard greens, and onion in the slow cooker.

3. In a medium bowl, whisk together the remaining 1 cup of broth, ginger, tomato paste, peanut butter, Sriracha, and salt. Stir this mixture into the slow cooker.

4. Cover and cook on low for 6 to 8 hours. Garnish each serving with fresh cilantro, a lime wedge, and the peanuts.

COOKING TIP If you prefer the texture of white rice, feel free to swap it for the brown rice and reduce the cooking time to 4 to 6 hours.

SUBSTITUTION TIP To ensure this recipe is Gluten-Free, use gluten-free low-sodium vegetable broth.

Vegetarian Cassoulet

Serves 2

Traditional French cassoulet is about as un-vegetarian as it gets. It's made with duck or chicken, sausage, and salt pork. This version of the rich casserole is a slow-simmering bean stew studded with flavorful, "meaty" bites that will appeal to both those who do and don't eat meat.

PREP
10 minutes

COOK
6 to 8 hours

1 teaspoon extra-virgin olive oil

2 (15-ounce) cans navy beans, drained and rinsed

16 ounces vegan sausage, cut into 1-inch pieces

1 cup minced onion

¼ cup minced celery

1 tablespoon minced garlic

1 teaspoon minced fresh sage

1 cup low-sodium vegetable broth

PER SERVING
Calories: 685
Saturated Fat: 0g
Trans Fat: 0g
Carbohydrates: 106g
Fiber: 38g
Sodium: 1251mg
Protein: 55g

1. Grease the inside of the slow cooker with the olive oil.

2. Put the beans, sausage, onion, celery, garlic, and sage in the slow cooker. Stir to mix thoroughly. Pour in the vegetable broth.

3. Cover and cook on low for 6 to 8 hours, until the beans are very tender but not falling apart.

COOKING TIP A variety of vegan sausage products exists on the market. Go with a mild-spiced sausage such as Field Roast's Smoked Apple Sage. Skip the Italian and chorizo-flavored products, which would dominate this mild dish.

SUBSTITUTION TIP To ensure this dish is Allergy Friendly and Gluten-Free, use gluten-free low-sodium vegetable broth.

five

Pork & Poultry

80 Chicken & Grape Tomatoes

81 Chicken & Artichoke Bake

82 Chicken in Mango Chutney

83 Chicken with
    Mushrooms & Shallots

84 Pesto Chicken with
    Stewed Vegetables

85 Chicken Pot Pie

86 Chicken Chili Verde
    over Rice

87 Sausage, Fennel & Chicken

88 Roasted Red Pepper &
    Mozzarella Stuffed
    Chicken Breasts

89 Chicken Fajitas

90 Coq au Vin Blanc

91 Cassoulet

92 Cashew Chicken & Snap Peas

93 Chicken Tikka Masala

94 Pork Chops with
    Apples & Onions

95 Pork Tenderloin with
    Rosemary Peaches

96 Balsamic-Glazed
    Pork Tenderloin & Carrots

97 Soy-Ginger Pork Chops
    with Green Beans

98 Cuban-Style Pork Street Tacos

99 Pork Chops with
    Mashed Sweet Potatoes

100 Cranberry-Glazed
    Pork Tenderloin

101 Carnitas with Avocado,
    Cilantro & Queso Fresco

HEART
HEALTHY

DIABETES
FRIENDLY

ALLERGY
FRIENDLY

GLUTEN-
FREE

LOW
CALORIE

PREP
10 minutes

COOK
8 hours

PER SERVING
Calories: 379
Saturated Fat: 0g
Trans Fat: 0g
Carbohydrates: 10g
Fiber: 3g
Sodium: 458mg
Protein: 28g

Chicken & Grape Tomatoes

Serves 2

This simple recipe is brimming with the flavors of the Mediterranean. I prefer the smaller, sweeter grape tomatoes, but if you cannot find them, use cherry tomatoes instead. Consider serving this dish with Cilantro Rice Pilaf (page 140) or Mediterranean Couscous (page 141).

1 pint grape tomatoes

4 garlic cloves, smashed

Zest of 1 lemon

1 teaspoon extra-virgin olive oil

2 bone-in, skinless chicken thighs, about 8 ounces each

1 teaspoon fresh thyme

½ teaspoon fresh rosemary

⅛ teaspoon sea salt

Freshly ground black pepper

1. Put the tomatoes, garlic, lemon zest, and olive oil in the slow cooker. Gently stir to mix.

2. Place the chicken thighs over the tomato mixture and season them with the thyme, rosemary, salt, and a few grinds of black pepper.

3. Cover and cook on low for 8 hours.

SUBSTITUTION TIP If you don't have fresh herbs on hand, use 1 teaspoon of herbes de Provence instead.

Chicken & Artichoke Bake

Serves 2

I once worked at an Italian restaurant where we served linguine with chicken, artichoke hearts, tomatoes, and smoked mozzarella. It was a customer favorite! This is my low-carbohydrate rendition of that delicious dish.

1 teaspoon extra-virgin olive oil

2 bone-in, skinless chicken breasts, about 8 ounces each

⅛ teaspoon sea salt

Freshly ground black pepper

1 (8-ounce) jar low-sodium artichoke hearts, drained

2 fresh tomatoes, diced

½ red onion, halved and sliced in thin rings

2 garlic cloves, minced

Zest of 1 lemon

Juice of 1 lemon

¼ cup fresh basil

2 tablespoons shredded smoked mozzarella, for garnish

1. Grease the inside of the slow cooker with the olive oil. Season the chicken breasts with the salt and pepper and put them into the slow cooker.

2. Add the artichoke hearts, tomatoes, onion, garlic, lemon zest, lemon juice, and basil on top of the chicken. Do not stir the ingredients.

3. Cover and cook on low for 6 to 8 hours, until the chicken is cooked through and the vegetables are very tender. Garnish each serving with 1 tablespoon smoked mozzarella.

SUBSTITUTION TIP For convenience, you can also purchase marinated artichoke hearts and omit the garlic and lemon.

PREP
10 minutes

COOK
6 to 8 hours

PER SERVING
Calories: 452
Saturated Fat: 5g
Trans Fat: 0g
Carbohydrates: 17g
Fiber: 4g
Sodium: 747mg
Protein: 54g

HEART
HEALTHY

DIABETES
FRIENDLY

ALLERGY
FRIENDLY

GLUTEN-
FREE

LOW
CALORIE

PREP
10 minutes

COOK
6 to 8 hours

PER SERVING
Calories: 405
Saturated Fat: 4g
Trans Fat: 0g
Carbohydrates: 20g
Fiber: 3g
Sodium: 267mg
Protein: 51g

Chicken in Mango Chutney

Serves 2

This sweet, tangy chutney dish is delicious served over steamed rice or on a bed of mixed greens. Make sure to use canned mango in this recipe; the enzymes in the raw fruit will break down the proteins in the chicken, similar to the enzymatic reaction of fresh pineapple.

12 ounces boneless, skinless chicken thighs, cut into 1-inch pieces

½ cup thinly sliced red onion

1 cup canned mango or peaches, drained and diced

2 tablespoons golden raisins

2 tablespoons apple cider vinegar

1 teaspoon minced fresh ginger

¼ teaspoon red pepper flakes

1 teaspoon curry powder

¼ teaspoon ground cinnamon

⅛ teaspoon sea salt

1. Put all the ingredients to the slow cooker and gently stir to combine.

2. Cover and cook on low for 6 to 8 hours. The chutney should be thick and sweet and the chicken tender and cooked through.

NUTRITION TIP Turmeric is what gives curry powder its brilliant yellow hue. The spice is rich in manganese and iron and has anti-inflammatory properties.

Chicken with Mushrooms & Shallots

Serves 2

HEART
HEALTHY

DIABETES
FRIENDLY

ALLERGY
FRIENDLY

GLUTEN-
FREE

LOW
CALORIE

PREP
10 minutes

COOK
6 to 8 hours

PER SERVING
Calories: 208
Saturated Fat: 2g
Trans Fat: 0g
Carbohydrates: 5g
Fiber: 1g
Sodium: 233mg
Protein: 24g

I love cooking with sherry, especially dry Spanish sherry, which my husband bought me from a trip to Spain. Like white and red wine, sherry adds complexity and flavor to a dish, and all the alcohol cooks out. Just make sure not to buy cooking sherry, which has tons of added salt.

1 teaspoon unsalted butter, at room temperature, or extra-virgin olive oil

2 cups thinly sliced cremini mushrooms

1 teaspoon fresh thyme

2 garlic cloves, minced

1 shallot, minced

3 tablespoons dry sherry

2 bone-in, skinless chicken thighs, about 6 ounces each

⅛ teaspoon sea salt

Freshly ground black pepper

1. Grease the inside of the slow cooker with the butter.

2. Put the mushrooms, thyme, garlic, and shallot into the slow cooker, tossing them gently to combine. Pour in the sherry.

3. Season the chicken with the salt and pepper and place the thighs on top of the mushroom mixture.

4. Cover and cook on low for 6 to 8 hours.

SUBSTITUTION TIP Cremini mushrooms are often labeled "baby bellas." If you cannot find them, you can use white button mushrooms as well.

PREP
10 minutes

COOK
6 to 8 hours

PER SERVING
Calories: 533
Saturated Fat: 8g
Trans Fat: 0g
Carbohydrates: 17g
Fiber: 6g
Sodium: 740mg
Protein: 33g

Pesto Chicken with Stewed Vegetables

Serves 2

I love the meltingly soft texture of stewed vegetables. Feel free to swap the zucchini for another favorite vegetable and use fresh herbs, such as thyme, rosemary, and oregano, or whatever you have on hand. This recipe isn't an exact science—it's about using whatever is fresh and seasonal.

1 zucchini, cut into 1-inch pieces

1 cup grape tomatoes

1 red bell pepper, cored and sliced thin

½ red onion, halved and sliced thin

1 tablespoon assorted fresh herbs

1 teaspoon extra-virgin olive oil

⅛ teaspoon sea salt

Freshly ground black pepper

2 bone-in, skinless chicken thighs, about 8 ounces each

¼ cup pesto

1. Put the zucchini, grape tomatoes, red bell pepper, onion, and herbs in the slow cooker and gently stir until mixed together. Drizzle the vegetables with the olive oil. Season with the salt and a few grinds of the black pepper.

2. In a medium bowl, coat the chicken on all sides with the pesto, then place the chicken on top of the vegetables.

3. Cover and cook on low for 6 to 8 hours until the vegetables are very tender and the chicken is cooked through.

COOKING TIP You can make your own pesto. In a blender or small food processor add 1 packed cup fresh basil, ¼ cup extra-virgin olive oil, 2 garlic cloves, 2 tablespoons toasted pine nuts, 1 teaspoon lemon juice, and a pinch of sea salt. Pulse until fairly smooth. This yields about 1 cup of pesto. Freeze leftovers in ice cube trays so you can remove just as much as you need!

Chicken Pot Pie

Serves 2

This low-carbohydrate chicken pot pie has everything you love about the classic version but without the crust. If you can't live without the carbohydrates, serve it alongside lightly buttered Whole-Grain Dinner Rolls (page 145) or spoon over Fluffy Buttermilk Biscuits (page 146). This dish is even more delightful with a chilled glass of white wine.

2 boneless, skinless chicken thighs, diced

1 cup diced, peeled Yukon Gold potatoes

1 cup frozen peas, thawed

1 cup diced onions

1 cup diced carrots

1 teaspoon fresh thyme

⅛ teaspoon sea salt

Freshly ground black pepper

1 tablespoon all-purpose flour

1 cup low-sodium chicken broth

1. Put the chicken, potatoes, peas, onions, carrots, and thyme in the slow cooker. Season with the salt and a few grinds of the pepper. Sprinkle in the flour and toss to coat the chicken and vegetables. Pour in the chicken broth.

2. Cover and cook on low for 8 hours.

NUTRITION TIP The taurine present in dark meat chicken has been shown to reduce the risk of coronary artery disease, perhaps due to its anti-inflammatory properties and ability to regulate blood pressure.

HEART
HEALTHY

DIABETES
FRIENDLY

LOW
CALORIE

PREP
10 minutes

COOK
8 hours

PER SERVING
Calories: 488
Saturated Fat: 6g
Trans Fat: 0g
Carbohydrates: 33g
Fiber: 8g
Sodium: 580mg
Protein: 35g

PORK & POULTRY

HEART
HEALTHY

DIABETES
FRIENDLY

ALLERGY
FRIENDLY

GLUTEN-
FREE

LOW
CALORIE

PREP
10 minutes

COOK
6 hours

PER SERVING
Calories: 527
Saturated Fat: 4g
Trans Fat: 0g
Carbohydrates: 44g
Fiber: 5g
Sodium: 469mg
Protein: 58g

Chicken Chili Verde over Rice

Serves 2

Once I found a whole bunch of tomatillos sitting on the giveaway table at the community garden near my apartment. I snatched them up quickly and trotted home to make salsa verde. I love the brightness of tomatillos in this classic green sauce.

1 cup diced tomatillos

1 onion, halved and sliced thin

2 garlic cloves, minced

1 jalapeño pepper, seeds and membranes removed, minced

1 teaspoon ground cumin

1 teaspoon ground coriander

1 teaspoon extra-virgin olive oil

½ cup long-grain brown rice

1 cup low-sodium chicken broth

2 boneless, skinless chicken breasts, about 8 ounces each, cut into 4-inch tenders

¼ cup fresh cilantro

1. Combine the tomatillos, onion, garlic, jalapeño, cumin, and coriander in a food processor. Pulse until it has a sauce-like consistency but is still slightly chunky.

2. Grease the inside of the slow cooker with the olive oil.

3. Add the rice to the slow cooker and pour in the chicken broth. Gently stir to make sure the rice grains are fully submerged.

4. Place the chicken on top of the rice and pour the tomatillo salsa over the top.

5. Cover and cook on low for 6 hours.

COOKING TIP You can find fresh tomatillos near the tomatoes in most supermarket produce aisles. They look like green tomatoes covered in papery green husks. Remove the husks and rinse the sticky residue from the fruits before using.

SUBSTITUTION TIP To ensure this recipe is Allergy Friendly and Gluten-Free, use gluten-free low-sodium vegetable broth.

Sausage, Fennel & Chicken

Serves 2

While this extravagant dish doesn't sound healthy, it's actually low in carbohydrates and is less than 350 calories per serving. If you're not carb averse, try it with Fluffy Buttermilk Biscuits (page 146) for a real treat.

½ fennel bulb, cored and sliced thin

½ red onion, halved and sliced thin

1 teaspoon extra-virgin olive oil

2 bone-in, skinless chicken thighs, about 8 ounces each

⅛ teaspoon sea salt

1 hot Italian sausage link, casing removed

1. Put the fennel, onion, and olive oil in the slow cooker. Gently stir to combine.

2. Season the chicken with the salt and set it atop the fennel and onion.

3. Crumble the sausage around the chicken.

4. Cover and cook on low for 8 hours.

COOKING TIP Look for Italian sausage without added sugar. There is some debate about whether nitrate- and nitrite-free cured meat is healthier. If you can find sausage made without these chemicals, you may wish to opt for it to be on the safe side.

PREP
10 minutes

COOK
8 hours

PER SERVING
Calories: 341
Saturated Fat: 1g
Trans Fat: 0g
Carbohydrates: 7g
Fiber: 2g
Sodium: 292mg
Protein: 24g

PORK & POULTRY

HEART
HEALTHY

DIABETES
FRIENDLY

LOW
CALORIE

GLUTEN-
FREE

PREP
10 minutes

COOK
6 to 8 hours

PER SERVING
Calories: 385
Saturated Fat: 6g
Trans Fat: 0g
Carbohydrates: 8g
Fiber: 3g
Sodium: 414mg
Protein: 50g

Roasted Red Pepper & Mozzarella Stuffed Chicken Breasts

Serves 2

This easy weeknight supper is brimming with flavor and requires virtually no effort. It's high in protein and low in carbohydrates. For a healthy, slimming side dish, serve with Simple Salad (page 134).

1 teaspoon extra-virgin olive oil

2 boneless, skinless chicken breasts

⅛ teaspoon sea salt

Freshly ground black pepper

2 roasted red bell peppers, cut into thin strips

2 ounces sliced mozzarella cheese

¼ cup roughly chopped fresh basil

1. Grease the inside of the slow cooker with the olive oil.

2. Slice the chicken breasts through the center horizontally until nearly sliced in half. Open as if opening a book. Season all sides of the chicken with the salt and pepper.

3. Place a layer of the roasted peppers on one inside half of each chicken breast. Top the peppers with the mozzarella slices. Then sprinkle the cheese with the fresh basil. Fold the other half of the chicken over the filling.

4. Carefully place the stuffed chicken breasts into the slow cooker, making sure the filling does not escape. Cover and cook on low for 6 to 8 hours, or until the chicken is cooked through.

VARIATION TIP For alternative flavors, swap the red bell peppers for marinated artichoke hearts, use Parmesan cheese instead of mozzarella, and use mint instead of basil.

Chicken Fajitas

Serves 2

I love fajitas but could live without the searing hot iron skillet being set in front of me, as so many restaurants present the dish. The slow cooker does a much better job—no spattering oil and no chance of second-degree burns. Bonus—these fajitas are also lower in fat.

1 onion, halved and sliced thin

3 sweet bell peppers, assorted colors, cored and sliced thin

½ teaspoon ground cumin

½ teaspoon smoked paprika

¼ teaspoon red pepper flakes

16 ounces boneless, skinless chicken breast, cut into 4-inch-long tenders

1 teaspoon extra-virgin olive oil

⅛ teaspoon sea salt

4 corn tortillas

¼ cup fresh cilantro, for garnish

1 small avocado, sliced, for garnish

1 lime, cut into wedges, for garnish

1. Put the onion, bell peppers, cumin, paprika, red pepper flakes, chicken, and olive oil in the slow cooker and toss to combine. Season the chicken and vegetables with the salt.

2. Cover and cook on low for 6 hours.

3. Serve the fajita mixture with warmed corn tortillas and garnished with the cilantro, avocado, and a generous squeeze of fresh lime juice.

COOKING TIP Warm the tortillas in a dry skillet, or directly on a gas stovetop flame over low heat. Use tongs to turn each tortilla, heating for a few seconds on each side until warm and pliable. They can also be warmed in the microwave, for 10 seconds each.

NUTRITION TIP Sweet bell peppers are rich in nutrients, but they can also be a dangerous source of pesticide residue. Purchase organic peppers whenever possible.

PREP
10 minutes

COOK
6 hours

PER SERVING
Calories: 680
Saturated Fat: 5g
Trans Fat: 0g
Carbohydrates: 50g
Fiber: 16g
Sodium: 272mg
Protein: 56g

HEART
HEALTHY

DIABETES
FRIENDLY

ALLERGY
FRIENDLY

GLUTEN-
FREE

LOW
CALORIE

PREP
10 minutes

COOK
8 hours

PER SERVING
Calories: 415
Saturated Fat: 0g
Trans Fat: 0g
Carbohydrates: 11g
Fiber: 2g
Sodium: 245mg
Protein: 51g

Coq au Vin Blanc

Serves 2

It doesn't get much simpler or more classic than chicken cooked in white wine, shallots, and herbs. I usually enjoy it with nothing more than a glass of the white wine that is also used in the dish, but if you need a starch, add a few peeled, diced potatoes to the recipe along with the onions and mushrooms.

1 teaspoon extra-virgin olive oil

2 bone-in, skinless chicken breasts, about 12 ounces each

1 cup blanched pearl onions

6 to 8 button mushrooms, quartered

1 teaspoon minced garlic

1 teaspoon fresh thyme

⅛ teaspoon sea salt

Freshly ground black pepper

1 cup dry white wine

1. Grease the inside of the slow cooker with the olive oil. Arrange the chicken in the bottom of the slow cooker. You may have to bend it slightly to fit; the breasts should not stack on top of each other.

2. Put the onions, mushroom, garlic, and thyme on top of the chicken. Season everything with the salt and a few grinds of the pepper. Pour in the wine.

3. Cover and cook on low for 8 hours.

COOKING TIP If you're in the mood for something decadent, make a classic French beurre blanc sauce to accompany the chicken. When the chicken is cooked, remove the chicken to a serving dish. Pour the wine and juices from the slow cooker into a skillet and heat over medium-low heat. Add 1 tablespoon minced shallot and cook for 5 to 7 minutes, until the liquid has reduced to just a few tablespoons. Remove the skillet from the heat and whisk in 3 tablespoons cold butter, 1 teaspoon at a time. Pour the thickened sauce over the chicken.

Cassoulet

HEART
HEALTHY

DIABETES
FRIENDLY

ALLERGY
FRIENDLY

GLUTEN-
FREE

LOW
CALORIE

The slow cooker provides a nearly authentic cooking vessel for this traditional French dish of beans, pork, and meat. This version gets a healthy upgrade using bone-in chicken thighs instead of duck confit, and just a hint of smoky flavor from the bacon.

1 cup navy beans, drained and rinsed

1 slice applewood-smoked bacon, cut into thin strips

1 small onion, halved and sliced thin

4 garlic cloves, smashed

1 teaspoon herbes de Provence

½ cup low-sodium chicken broth

2 bone-in, skinless chicken thighs, about 8 ounces each

⅛ teaspoon sea salt

Freshly ground black pepper

PREP
10 minutes

COOK
8 hours

PER SERVING
Calories: 514
Saturated Fat: 1g
Trans Fat: 0g
Carbohydrates: 26g
Fiber: 8g
Sodium: 348mg
Protein: 39g

1. Put the beans, bacon, onion, garlic, herbes de Provence, and broth in the slow cooker and stir until thoroughly mixed. Set the chicken pieces on top of the beans. Season with the salt and a few grinds of the black pepper.

2. Cover and cook on low for 8 hours.

NUTRITION TIP Navy beans are a good source of fiber and protein as well as folate, vitamin B, manganese, copper, phosphorus, iron, and magnesium.

SUBSTITUTION TIP To ensure this is Allergy Friendly and Gluten-Free, use gluten-free low-sodium vegetable broth.

PREP
10 minutes

COOK
6 hours

PER SERVING
Calories: 419
Saturated Fat: 2g
Trans Fat: 0g
Carbohydrates: 18g
Fiber: 3g
Sodium: 1086mg
Protein: 54g

Cashew Chicken & Snap Peas

Serves 2

It's the sweet, sour, and spicy sauce that will make you want more of this classic Chinese takeout recipe. When you have control of the ingredients, you can skip the food additives such as monosodium glutamate (MSG). This dish is nice on its own for a low-carbohydrate meal or served with steamed rice.

16 ounces boneless, skinless chicken breasts, cut into 2-inch pieces

2 cups sugar snap peas, strings removed

1 teaspoon grated fresh ginger

1 teaspoon minced garlic

2 tablespoons low-sodium soy sauce

1 tablespoon ketchup

1 tablespoon rice vinegar

1 teaspoon honey

Pinch red pepper flakes

¼ cup toasted cashews

1 scallion, white and green parts, sliced thin

1. Put the chicken and sugar snap peas into the slow cooker.

2. In a measuring cup or small bowl, whisk together the ginger, garlic, soy sauce, ketchup, vinegar, honey, and red pepper flakes. Pour the mixture over the chicken and snap peas.

3. Cover and cook on low for 6 hours. The chicken should be cooked through, and the snap peas should be tender, but not mushy.

4. Just before serving, stir in the cashews and scallions.

NUTRITION TIP Cashews are a wonderful source of copper, with nearly 100 percent of your daily value in just ¼ cup. They are also rich in phosphorus, manganese, magnesium, and zinc.

SUBSTITUTION TIP To ensure this is Gluten-Free, use gluten-free low-sodium soy sauce.

Chicken Tikka Masala

Serves 2

HEART
HEALTHY

DIABETES
FRIENDLY

ALLERGY
FRIENDLY

GLUTEN-
FREE

LOW
CALORIE

The slow cooker provides a great vessel for preparing both traditional foods and those with more complex flavors. This easy tikka masala is brimming with the spices of India. Serve with flat-bread or Simple Salad (page 134).

16 ounces boneless, skinless chicken breast

1 cup diced onion

1 cup diced fresh tomatoes

1 teaspoon ground coriander

1 teaspoon ground cumin

1 teaspoon smoked paprika

⅛ teaspoon red pepper flakes

1 teaspoon minced fresh ginger

1 cup low-sodium chicken broth

2 tablespoons heavy cream or coconut cream

¼ cup minced fresh cilantro, for garnish

1. Put the chicken, onion, tomatoes, coriander, cumin, paprika, red pepper flakes, ginger, and chicken broth in the slow cooker. Stir to combine the ingredients.

2. Cover and cook on low for 6 hours, until the chicken is cooked through and the tomatoes and onions are soft.

3. Allow the dish to rest in the slow cooker, uncovered, for 10 minutes, then stir in the heavy cream. Garnish each serving with the cilantro.

COOKING TIP The fat in heavy cream acts as a stabilizer, making the cream less likely to curdle when added to hot food.

SUBSTITUTION TIP To ensure this dish is Gluten-Free, use gluten-free low-sodium chicken broth, and use the coconut cream instead of the heavy cream to make it Allergy Friendly.

PREP
10 minutes

COOK
6 hours

PER SERVING
Calories: 368
Saturated Fat: 4g
Trans Fat: 0g
Carbohydrates: 12g
Fiber: 3g
Sodium: 166mg
Protein: 51g

HEART
HEALTHY

DIABETES
FRIENDLY

ALLERGY
FRIENDLY

GLUTEN-
FREE

LOW
CALORIE

PREP
10 minutes

COOK
6 to 8 hours

PER SERVING
Calories: 286
Saturated Fat: 5g
Trans Fat: 0g
Carbohydrates: 22g
Fiber: 4g
Sodium: 521mg
Protein: 21g

Pork Chops with Apples & Onions

Serves 2

The apples and onions in this recipe cook down into a thick, comforting compote, which is served on top of the pork chops. Simple Salad (page 134) complements this dish well.

1 apple, cored, peeled, and cut into 8 wedges

1 sweet onion, cut into thick rings

1 teaspoon fresh thyme

¼ teaspoon ground cinnamon

¼ cup apple cider

2 bone-in pork chops

⅛ teaspoon sea salt

Freshly ground black pepper

1. Put the apple, onion, thyme, and cinnamon in the slow cooker and stir to combine. Pour in the apple cider.

2. Season the pork chops with the salt and a few grinds of the black pepper. Set the chops atop the apple and onion mixture.

3. Cover and cook on low for 6 to 8 hours, until the apples and onion are very soft and the pork is cooked through.

COOKING TIP As with any meat cooked in a slow cooker, the flavor of the pork is improved if you first brown it on all sides in a skillet in just a bit of extra-virgin olive oil.

Pork Tenderloin with Rosemary Peaches

Serves 2

HEART
HEALTHY

DIABETES
FRIENDLY

ALLERGY
FRIENDLY

GLUTEN-
FREE

LOW
CALORIE

Peaches and rosemary are two of my favorite summer flavors. But you can enjoy this dish year round by using frozen peaches. Just be sure to defrost the fruit completely before adding it to the slow cooker. Consider serving with Fluffy Buttermilk Biscuits (page 146).

2 peaches, peeled and cut into wedges

½ red onion, halved and sliced thin

1 sprig rosemary, needles only

16 ounces pork tenderloin

⅛ teaspoon sea salt

Freshly ground black pepper

1. Put the peaches, onion, and rosemary needles in the slow cooker and stir to combine.

2. Season the pork tenderloin with the salt and a few grinds of the black pepper. Set the tenderloin on top of the peach and onion mixture.

3. Cover and cook on low for 6 to 8 hours, until the onion and fruit has softened and the pork is tender and cooked through.

NUTRITION TIP Pork isn't typically thought of as a health food, but it is a good source of lean protein and is rich in thiamin, selenium, niacin, vitamin B_6, and phosphorus.

PREP
10 minutes

COOK
6 to 8 hours

PER SERVING
Calories: 374
Saturated Fat: 3g
Trans Fat: 0g
Carbohydrates: 12g
Fiber: 2g
Sodium: 247mg
Protein: 61g

PORK & POULTRY

HEART
HEALTHY

DIABETES
FRIENDLY

ALLERGY
FRIENDLY

GLUTEN-
FREE

LOW
CALORIE

PREP
10 minutes

COOK
6 to 8 hours

PER SERVING
Calories: 400
Saturated Fat: 3g
Trans Fat: 0g
Carbohydrates: 16g
Fiber: 4g
Sodium: 351mg
Protein: 61g

Balsamic-Glazed Pork Tenderloin & Carrots

Serves 2

I love the flavors of onion, carrots, and balsamic vinegar in this recipe. The long, slow cooking allows the sugars in the vegetables to intensify. They're offset beautifully by the tangy balsamic vinegar and the richness of the pork tenderloin.

½ red onion, halved and sliced thin

4 carrots, cut into 2-inch pieces

2 garlic cloves, minced

16 ounces pork tenderloin

⅛ teaspoon sea salt

Freshly ground black pepper

¼ cup balsamic vinegar

½ cup low-sodium chicken or vegetable broth

1. Put the onion, carrots, and garlic in the slow cooker and stir to combine.

2. Season the pork tenderloin with the salt and a few grinds of the black pepper. Set the tenderloin on top of the vegetables. Pour the vinegar and broth over the meat.

3. Cover and cook on low for 6 to 8 hours, until the vegetables are tender and the meat is cooked through.

COOKING TIP Keep chicken broth on hand at all times by freezing it in ice cube trays and storing the cubes in a sealed container. Defrost only what you need for each recipe.

SUBSTITUTION TIP To ensure this is Allergy Friendly and Gluten-Free, use gluten-free low-sodium vegetable broth.

Soy-Ginger Pork Chops with Green Beans

==== Serves 2 ====

Layering the pork on the bottom of the slow cooker allows the meat to cook in the liquid and become very tender while the green beans gently steam. If you're looking for a few more calories, serve with steamed rice. Otherwise, enjoy this healthy, low-carbohydrate meal on its own.

PREP
10 minutes

COOK
8 hours

PER SERVING
Calories: 333
Saturated Fat: 4g
Trans Fat: 0g
Carbohydrates: 17g
Fiber: 6g
Sodium: 2498mg
Protein: 35g

1 teaspoon extra-virgin olive oil

2 bone-in pork chops, about 8 ounces each

Freshly ground black pepper

3 cups whole green beans, stems removed

2 teaspoons minced fresh ginger

1 teaspoon minced garlic

¼ cup low-sodium soy sauce

½ cup low-sodium chicken or vegetable broth

1. Grease the inside of the slow cooker with the olive oil.

2. Put the pork chops in the bottom of the crock and season them with a few grinds of the black pepper. Place the green beans on top of the pork.

3. In a small bowl, whisk together the ginger, garlic, soy sauce, and broth. Pour this mixture over the green beans and pork.

4. Cover and cook on low for 8 hours, until the pork is cooked through and the green beans are tender.

NUTRITION TIP Green beans are rich in vitamin K, manganese, B vitamins, and the mineral silicon.

SUBSTITUTION TIP To ensure this dish is Gluten-Free, use gluten-free low-sodium soy sauce and chicken broth.

HEART
HEALTHY

DIABETES
FRIENDLY

ALLERGY
FRIENDLY

GLUTEN-
FREE

LOW
CALORIE

PREP
10 minutes

COOK
8 hours

PER SERVING
Calories: 510
Saturated Fat: 3g
Trans Fat: 0g
Carbohydrates: 34g
Fiber: 7g
Sodium: 308mg
Protein: 64g

Cuban-Style Pork Street Tacos

Serves 2

The bright flavor of coriander and citrus-infused pork, onions, and peppers provides the perfect filling for "street" tacos. Include beans, avocado, and sour cream as garnishes if you need more energy or you are serving these tacos to guests.

1 teaspoon extra-virgin olive oil

16 ounces pork tenderloin

Zest of 1 orange

Juice of 1 orange

Zest of 1 lime

Juice of 1 lime

2 garlic cloves, minced

1 teaspoon ground cumin

1 teaspoon ground coriander

⅛ teaspoon sea salt

Freshly ground black pepper

1 red onion, halved and sliced thin

1 red bell pepper, cored and sliced thin

1 green bell pepper, cored and sliced thin

4 corn tortillas

¼ cup fresh cilantro, for garnish

1. Grease the inside of the slow cooker with the olive oil.

2. Put the pork tenderloin in the slow cooker.

3. In a small measuring cup, whisk together the orange zest, orange juice, lime zest, lime juice, garlic, cumin, coriander, salt, and a few grinds of the black pepper. Pour this mixture over the pork.

4. Put the onion, red bell pepper, and green bell pepper in the crock, placing them around and on top of the pork.

5. Cover and cook on low for 8 hours.

6. Remove the pork from the slow cooker and allow the meat to rest for 10 minutes before shredding it with a fork. Return it to the slow cooker and toss it with the vegetables and juices.

7. Serve the pork in warm corn tortillas garnished with the cilantro.

COOKING TIP Warm the tortillas in a dry skillet, or directly on a gas stovetop flame over low heat. Use tongs to turn each tortilla, heating for a few seconds on each side until warm and pliable. They can also be warmed in the microwave, for 10 seconds each.

NUTRITION TIP Fresh cilantro, also called coriander, is one of the most widely used herbs around the globe. Fresh coriander leaves have detoxifying properties and ground coriander seed has anti-inflammatory properties.

Pork Chops with Mashed Sweet Potatoes

Serves 2

HEART
HEALTHY

DIABETES
FRIENDLY

ALLERGY
FRIENDLY

GLUTEN-
FREE

LOW
CALORIE

One year over Christmas I was asked to make the sweet potatoes. I knew the obvious answer involved marshmallows, brown sugar, and butter. But I wanted a healthier option, and came up with these savory mashed sweet potatoes with a hint of nutmeg and orange. Even the kids love them!

2 sweet potatoes, peeled and diced

Zest of 1 orange

Pinch ground nutmeg

½ cup low-sodium chicken broth

2 bone-in pork chops, about 8 ounces each

Sea salt

Freshly ground black pepper

PREP
10 minutes

COOK
6 to 8 hours

PER SERVING
Calories: 529
Saturated Fat: 7g
Trans Fat: 0g
Carbohydrates: 44g
Fiber: 7g
Sodium: 163mg
Protein: 36g

1. Put the sweet potatoes, orange zest, nutmeg, and broth into the slow cooker. Gently stir together.

2. Season the pork chops with the salt and black pepper and set them on top of the sweet potatoes.

3. Cover and cook on low for 6 to 8 hours, until the sweet potatoes are completely soft and the pork is cooked through.

4. If any large sweet potato chunks remain, mash them with a potato masher or the back of a fork before serving.

SUBSTITUTION TIP To ensure this recipe is Allergy Friendly and Gluten-Free, use gluten-free low-sodium vegetable broth.

COOKING TIP Before eating an orange, I zest the peel with a grater or zester, and then I freeze the zest in a small zip-top bag until I need it.

HEART
HEALTHY

DIABETES
FRIENDLY

ALLERGY
FRIENDLY

GLUTEN-
FREE

PREP
10 minutes

COOK
8 hours

PER SERVING
Calories: 612
Saturated Fat: 3g
Trans Fat: 0g
Carbohydrates: 59g
Fiber: 10g
Sodium: 340mg
Protein: 63g

Cranberry-Glazed Pork Tenderloin

Serves 2

While cranberry sauce is usually thought of as a holiday condiment, it makes a simple and tasty glaze for meat any time of the year. Consider serving with Whole-Grain Dinner Rolls (page 145) or Fluffy Buttermilk Biscuits (page 146).

16 ounces pork tenderloin

⅛ teaspoon sea salt

Freshly ground black pepper

1 cup prepared cranberry sauce

½ cup low-sodium chicken broth

2 Belgian endives, halved

1 teaspoon extra-virgin olive oil

1. Season the pork with the salt and a few grinds of the black pepper and put in the slow cooker. Pour the cranberry sauce and chicken broth over the top of the tenderloin.

2. Place the endive over the pork, cut side up, and drizzle it with the olive oil.

3. Cover and cook on low for 8 hours.

COOKING TIP You can easily make your own cranberry sauce at home. Simply combine 12 ounces fresh cranberries, 1 cup water, the zest of 1 orange, and ¼ cup granulated sugar or honey in a medium saucepan. Cook over medium-low heat until thick and syrupy, about 10 minutes.

SUBSTITUTION TIP To ensure this recipe is Allergy Friendly and Gluten-Free, use gluten-free low-sodium vegetable broth.

Carnitas with Avocado, Cilantro & Queso Fresco

Serves 2

GLUTEN-FREE

LOW CALORIE

PREP
10 minutes

COOK
8 hours

PER SERVING
Calories: 581
Saturated Fat: 11g
Trans Fat: 0g
Carbohydrates: 32g
Fiber: 8g
Sodium: 340mg
Protein: 33g

The slow cooker does the heavy lifting for you in this flavorful Mexico City-inspired taco. Simply serve the filling with corn tortillas, fresh cilantro, and mild queso fresco. If you cannot find queso fresco, use crumbled mozzarella or good quality ricotta, but do not opt for cotija, which is very salty and can be overpowering. Or, save calories and use a fresh pico de gallo salsa.

1 teaspoon extra-virgin olive oil

1 teaspoon ground cumin

½ teaspoon ground coriander

1 teaspoon garlic powder

⅛ teaspoon sea salt

Freshly ground black pepper

10 ounces boneless pork shoulder roast

1 cup low-sodium chicken broth or water

1 tablespoon lime juice

4 corn tortillas

¼ cup diced red onions, for garnish

½ avocado, thinly sliced, for garnish

2 tablespoons crumbled queso fresco, for garnish

¼ cup roughly chopped fresh cilantro, for garnish

1. Grease the inside of the slow cooker crock with the oil.

2. Combine the cumin, coriander, garlic powder, salt, and pepper in a small bowl. Season the pork with this mixture and then place the meat into the slow cooker. Pour the broth around the meat, but not over it or the seasoning will wash off.

3. Cover and cook on low for 8 hours, until the meat is easily shredded with a fork. After the pork is shredded (this can be done in the slow cooker), stir in the lime juice.

4. To serve, divide the meat between the tortillas and garnish each with the onions, avocado, queso fresco, and cilantro.

COOKING TIP This recipe is perfect for doubling to make leftovers or to serve a crowd on game day. Warm the tortillas in a dry skillet, or directly on a gas stovetop flame over low heat. Use tongs to turn each tortilla, heating for a few seconds on each side until warm and pliable. They can also be warmed in the microwave, for 10 seconds each.

six

Beef & Lamb

104 Shepherd's Pie

105 Meatloaf

106 Ground Beef–Stuffed Bell Peppers

107 Beef Goulash with Pumpkin, Mushrooms & Pumpkin Seeds

108 Pot Roast

109 Beef Broccoli

110 Balsamic-Glazed Beef with Red Cabbage

111 Beef Ragù

112 Spiced Pot Roast with Celery & Mushrooms

113 Greek-Style Lamb Shoulder & Lemon Potatoes

114 Spanish-Style Lamb Chops

115 Korean-Style Short Ribs & Carrots

116 Osso Buco

117 Adobo Steak Fajitas

118 Irish-Style Lamb Stew

119 Honey-Soy Lamb & Rice

HEART
HEALTHY

DIABETES
FRIENDLY

GLUTEN-
FREE

LOW
CALORIE

PREP
10 minutes

COOK
8 hours

PER SERVING
Calories: 468
Saturated Fat: 6g
Trans Fat: 0g
Carbohydrates: 42g
Fiber: 8g
Sodium: 403mg
Protein: 45g

Shepherd's Pie

Serves 2

Shepherd's Pie is similar to meatloaf but the side dishes you might normally enjoy with meatloaf—peas and potatoes—are incorporated into the mixture. To reduce the fat and simultaneously improve the flavor of this recipe, season the meat with a pinch of salt and pepper and brown it in a large skillet over medium-high heat. When it is cooked through, drain the fat using a fine mesh sieve. Do not rinse the browned beef under running water.

8 ounces lean ground beef

1 cup frozen peas, thawed

1 cup diced carrots

½ cup diced onions

⅛ teaspoon sea salt

Freshly ground black pepper

1½ cups prepared mashed potatoes

2 tablespoons shredded sharp Cheddar cheese

1. Put the beef, peas, carrots, and onions in the slow cooker and stir together thoroughly. Season the mixture with the salt and a few grinds of the black pepper.

2. Spread the prepared mashed potatoes over the meat and vegetable mixture in an even layer.

3. Cover and cook on low for 8 hours.

4. Sprinkle the top of the shepherd's pie with the Cheddar cheese just before serving.

SUBSTITUTION TIP To make this recipe dairy-free, replace the milk and butter with unsweetened almond milk and a non-dairy butter substitute. Use a non-dairy cheese or omit it from the recipe all together.

COOKING TIP Have leftover homemade mashed potatoes from another meal? That's a good excuse for making shepherd's pie. Or, if you have instant potato flakes on hand, heat 1 cup water, 1 teaspoon butter, and ½ cup 2% milk in a small pot over medium heat until it comes to the barest simmer. Stir in 1 cup potato flakes and mix until just combined.

Meatloaf

Serves 2

Meatloaf is one of my favorite meals to make on evenings when my husband is working and I'm home with the kids. This makes the perfect amount for me and the boys, ages 4 and 8, and I can spend the afternoon with them while the meatloaf cooks. To make this dish gluten-free, make or use gluten-free bread crumbs.

PER SERVING
Calories: 525
Saturated Fat: 5g
Trans Fat: 0g
Carbohydrates: 36g
Fiber: 4g
Sodium: 783mg
Protein: 57g

8 ounces lean ground beef

4 ounces ground turkey

½ cup whole-grain bread crumbs

½ cup minced onion

1 teaspoon minced garlic

¼ cup minced fresh parsley

1 teaspoon minced fresh thyme

¼ cup ketchup

1 egg

⅛ teaspoon sea salt

Freshly ground black pepper

1 teaspoon extra-virgin olive oil

1. In a large bowl, combine the ground beef, ground turkey, bread crumbs, onion, garlic, parsley, thyme, ketchup, egg, salt, and a few grinds of the black pepper. Use your hands to mix all the ingredients together thoroughly.

2. Grease the inside of the slow cooker with the olive oil. Put the meatloaf mixture in the crock and form it into a loaf-like shape.

3. Cover and cook on low for 8 hours.

COOKING TIP Choose a ketchup without high-fructose corn syrup. High-fructose corn syrup has been linked to a wide array of health problems, including metabolic syndrome.

HEART
HEALTHY

DIABETES
FRIENDLY

LOW
CALORIE

PREP
10 minutes

COOK
8 hours

PER SERVING
Calories: 438
Saturated Fat: 6g
Trans Fat: 0g
Carbohydrates: 27g
Fiber: 7g
Sodium: 314mg
Protein: 46g

Ground Beef–Stuffed Bell Peppers

Serves 2

This recipe has many of the flavors you love in a lasagna, but without the copious amounts of saturated fat and carbohydrates. Consider serving the peppers with Simple Salad (page 134) and a glass of red wine.

1 teaspoon extra-virgin olive oil

4 narrow red bell peppers

8 ounces lean ground beef

½ cup diced onion

1 teaspoon ground fennel seed

1 teaspoon minced garlic

1 tablespoon Italian herb blend

2 tablespoons tomato paste

1 egg, beaten

2 tablespoons bread crumbs

¼ cup grated Parmesan cheese

1. Grease the inside of the slow cooker with olive oil.

2. Cut the tops off each of the red peppers and set the tops to the side. Remove the seeds and membranes from the interior of each pepper.

3. In a large bowl, add the beef, onion, fennel, garlic, Italian herb blend, tomato paste, egg, bread crumbs, and Parmesan cheese. Use your hands to mix the ingredients together thoroughly. Stuff the mixture into each of the peppers. Stand the peppers upright in the slow cooker, and place the tops on each pepper.

4. Cover and cook on low for 8 hours.

COOKING TIP None of the recipes in this book require precooking. However, to remove some of the fat from this dish, brown the meat in a skillet and drain the fat before combining the meat with the other ingredients.

Beef Goulash with Pumpkin, Mushrooms & Pumpkin Seeds

Serves 2

This hearty beef stew is perfect for fall. It combines the sweet spices of cinnamon and allspice with savory flavors of bay leaf and thyme. The pumpkin seeds (also called pepitas) add an interesting texture and a slight crunch. It is a complete meal on its own, but it's also tasty served with Whole-Grain Dinner Rolls (page 145).

12 ounces beef stew meat, cut into 1-inch cubes

1 small pie pumpkin or butternut squash, peeled and cut into 1-inch cubes

1 cup quartered button mushrooms

½ yellow onion, halved and cut into thin half circles

1 garlic clove, minced

¼ teaspoon ground cinnamon

⅛ teaspoon ground allspice

1 bay leaf

1 fresh thyme sprig

⅛ teaspoon sea salt

1 cup chicken broth

2 tablespoons pumpkin seeds

1. Put the beef, squash, mushrooms, onion, garlic, cinnamon, allspice, bay leaf, thyme sprig, salt, and broth into the slow cooker. Stir gently to mix.

2. Cover and cook on low for 8 hours. Remove the thyme sprig and bay leaf from the goulash before serving.

3. Garnish each serving with the pumpkin seeds.

COOKING TIP Kabocha squash can also be used in place of the pumpkin.

SUBSTITUTION TIP to ensure this dish is Allergy Friendly and Gluten-Free, use gluten-free chicken broth.

HEART HEALTHY

DIABETES FRIENDLY

ALLERGY FRIENDLY

GLUTEN-FREE

LOW CALORIE

PREP
10 minutes

COOK
8 hours

PER SERVING
Calories: 508
Saturated Fat: 5g
Trans Fat: 0g
Carbohydrates: 31g
Fiber: 7g
Sodium: 622mg
Protein: 61g

BEEF & LAMB

HEART
HEALTHY

DIABETES
FRIENDLY

ALLERGY
FRIENDLY

GLUTEN-
FREE

PREP
10 minutes

COOK
8 hours

PER SERVING
Calories: 696
Saturated Fat: 7g
Trans Fat: 0g
Carbohydrates: 46g
Fiber: 7g
Sodium: 524mg
Protein: 81g

Pot Roast

Serves 2

Meat and potatoes are about as comforting as food gets. For a few more vegetables, serve this dish with Simple Salad (page 134).

16 ounces chuck roast, trimmed of visible fat

⅛ teaspoon sea salt

Freshly ground black pepper

1 onion, cut into 8 wedges

2 carrots, cut into 2-inch pieces

2 red potatoes, quartered

1 teaspoon minced rosemary

1 cup low-sodium beef broth

1. Season the roast with the salt and a few grinds of the black pepper. Put it into the slow cooker. Arrange the onion, carrots, potatoes, and rosemary around the sides and on top of the meat.

2. Pour in the beef broth.

3. Cover and cook on low for 8 hours. The meat should be meltingly tender.

NUTRITION TIP Beef chuck is a relatively lean cut of meat, with only 15 grams of fat per pound and over 100 grams of protein. It is a good source of niacin, phosphorus, B vitamins, zinc, and selenium.

SUBSTITUTION TIP To ensure the roast is Allergy Friendly and Gluten-Free, use gluten-free low-sodium beef broth.

Beef Broccoli

Serves 2

This Chinese takeout–inspired recipe is healthy and delicious. For a refreshing accompaniment, consider serving it with Simple Salad (page 134).

12 ounces flank steak, sliced thin

2 cups broccoli florets

½ cup low-sodium beef broth

2 tablespoons low-sodium soy sauce

2 tablespoons honey or maple syrup

1 teaspoon toasted sesame oil

1 teaspoon minced garlic

1 tablespoon cornstarch

1. Put the flank steak and broccoli into the slow cooker.

2. In a measuring cup or small bowl, whisk together the beef broth, soy sauce, honey, sesame oil, garlic, and cornstarch. Pour this mixture over the beef and broccoli.

3. Cover and cook on low for 6 hours.

NUTRITION TIP Broccoli is a nutritional powerhouse. It is rich in vitamin K, vitamin C, potassium, chromium, copper, manganese, phosphorus, choline, and B vitamins.

SUBSTITUTION TIP To ensure the dish is Gluten-Free, use gluten-free low-sodium beef broth and soy sauce.

PREP
10 minutes

COOK
6 hours

PER SERVING
Calories: 471
Saturated Fat: 6g
Trans Fat: 0g
Carbohydrates: 29g
Fiber: 3g
Sodium: 1107mg
Protein: 52g

HEART
HEALTHY

DIABETES
FRIENDLY

ALLERGY
FRIENDLY

GLUTEN-
FREE

LOW
CALORIE

PREP
5 minutes

COOK
8 hours

PER SERVING
Calories: 382
Saturated Fat: 4g
Trans Fat: 0g
Carbohydrates: 8g
Fiber: 3g
Sodium: 276mg
Protein: 53g

Balsamic-Glazed Beef with Red Cabbage

Serves 2

Stewed beef and cabbage with mustard has a gratifying "old country" taste to it. Make sure to layer the ingredients into the slow cooker as indicated. This allows the beef to stew and the cabbage to steam gently.

12 ounces beef stew meat, trimmed of excess fat and cut into 1-inch pieces

2 cups shredded red cabbage

½ cup thinly sliced red onion

¼ cup dry red wine

¼ cup balsamic vinegar

1 teaspoon Dijon mustard

1 teaspoon ground cumin

⅛ teaspoon sea salt

Freshly ground black pepper

1. Put the beef in the bottom of the slow cooker and top it with the cabbage and then the onions.

2. In a large measuring cup or small bowl, whisk together the wine, vinegar, mustard, cumin, salt, and a few grinds of the black pepper. Pour this mixture into the slow cooker.

3. Cover and cook on low for 8 hours.

NUTRITION TIP Steamed cabbage is rich in a particular kind of fiber that binds to bile acids and may help lower cholesterol.

Beef Ragù

Serves 2

This is a great recipe to make when you're expecting guests or to have leftovers. Simply double all the ingredients except the stock, wine, and vinegar. Otherwise consider serving it as a delightfully messy sandwich on Whole-Grain Dinner Rolls (page 145).

16 ounces beef brisket, cut into two 8-ounce pieces

½ cup diced onion

1 teaspoon minced fresh rosemary

1 garlic clove, minced

¼ cup diced carrot

1 plum tomato, diced

1 cup low-sodium beef broth

½ cup dry red wine

1 tablespoon red wine vinegar

1 teaspoon tomato paste

¼ teaspoon sea salt

1. Combine all the ingredients in the slow cooker.

2. Cover and cook on low for 8 to 10 hours, or until the meat is very tender.

3. Transfer the brisket to a cutting board and shred it with a fork. Return it to the crock and stir it into the liquid to soak in even more flavor.

COOKING TIP For extra flavor, brown the beef brisket with a little extra-virgin olive oil in a large skillet over medium-high heat before placing it in the slow cooker.

SUBSTITUTION TIP To ensure the ragù is Allergy Friendly and Gluten-Free, use gluten-free low-sodium beef broth.

HEART HEALTHY

DIABETES FRIENDLY

ALLERGY FRIENDLY

GLUTEN-FREE

LOW CALORIE

PREP
10 minutes

COOK
8 to 10 hours

PER SERVING
Calories: 509
Saturated Fat: 5g
Trans Fat: 0g
Carbohydrates: 9g
Fiber: 2g
Sodium: 602mg
Protein: 71g

HEART
HEALTHY

DIABETES
FRIENDLY

ALLERGY
FRIENDLY

GLUTEN-
FREE

LOW
CALORIE

PREP
10 minutes

COOK
8 hours

PER SERVING
Calories: 586
Saturated Fat: 7g
Trans Fat: 0g
Carbohydrates: 15g
Fiber: 3g
Sodium: 528mg
Protein: 79g

Spiced Pot Roast with Celery & Mushrooms

Serves 2

Meltingly tender pot roast is a labor of love—usually. Here it is, with all the love but much less of the labor. The slow cooker gives the succulent texture you crave without demanding you repeatedly check the oven to make sure the roast doesn't dry out. If you have the time, rub the meat in the garlic and spice mixture overnight and then put it in the slow cooker in the morning with the vegetables.

1 teaspoon minced garlic

1 tablespoon tomato paste

¼ teaspoon ground allspice

⅛ teaspoon sea salt

Freshly ground black pepper

16 ounces beef chuck roast, trimmed of excess fat

2 carrots, cut into 2-inch pieces

1 celery stalk, cut into 2-inch pieces

2 shallots, peeled and halved

8 cremini mushrooms, halved

1 sprig fresh thyme

1 cup low-sodium beef broth

¼ cup dry red wine

1. In a small bowl, mix together the garlic, tomato paste, allspice, salt, and a few grinds of the black pepper. Rub the mixture all over the chuck roast, and then place it in the slow cooker.

2. Add the carrots, celery, shallots, mushrooms, and thyme to the slow cooker. Pour in the broth and wine.

3. Cover and cook on low for 8 hours.

VARIATION TIP If you prefer not to cook with wine, substitute with additional beef stock and add 1 teaspoon of apple cider vinegar.

SUBSTITUTION TIP To ensure this dish is Allergy Friendly and Gluten-Free, use gluten-free low-sodium beef broth.

Greek-Style Lamb Shoulder & Lemon Potatoes

Serves 2

My dad's wife, Maria, returns regularly to a small island in Greece where her relatives run a taverna. I can almost smell the food as she describes it to us. Until I have the chance to visit, I'll content myself by making Greek-style dishes, including this lamb shoulder infused with lemon, garlic, and herbs.

4 garlic cloves, minced, divided

Juice of 1 lemon

1 tablespoon minced fresh rosemary

1 tablespoon minced fresh oregano

½ teaspoon ground cinnamon

¼ teaspoon ground cumin

⅛ teaspoon sea salt

Freshly ground black pepper

2 bone-in lamb shoulder chops, about 6 ounces each, trimmed of excess fat

4 red potatoes, halved

Zest of 1 lemon

1 tablespoon extra-virgin olive oil

1. In a small bowl, mix together half of the garlic and the lemon juice, rosemary, oregano, cinnamon, cumin, salt, and a few grinds of the black pepper. Coat the lamb chops with this mixture and set aside; you can do this the night before if you wish.

2. Put the potatoes in the slow cooker along with the remaining garlic, lemon zest, and olive oil. Set the lamb shoulder atop the potatoes.

3. Cover and cook on low for 8 to 10 hours, until the lamb is tender and falling off the bone.

NUTRITION TIP Trying to cut back on sodium? Fresh herbs are your new best friend. They add loads of flavor and healthy micronutrients without the sodium in salt. Dried herbs will work in a pinch; simply use half of the amount of fresh herbs called for.

PREP
10 minutes

COOK
8 to 10 hours

PER SERVING
Calories: 540
Saturated Fat: 3g
Trans Fat: 0g
Carbohydrates: 68g
Fiber: 10g
Sodium: 226mg
Protein: 32g

BEEF & LAMB

HEART
HEALTHY

DIABETES
FRIENDLY

ALLERGY
FRIENDLY

GLUTEN-
FREE

LOW
CALORIE

PREP
10 minutes

COOK
8 hours

PER SERVING
Calories: 419
Saturated Fat: 4g
Trans Fat: 0g
Carbohydrates: 43g
Fiber: 6g
Sodium: 326mg
Protein: 27g

Spanish-Style Lamb Chops

Serves 2

Pairing lamb with bold spices makes me swoon. These lamb chops are coated in a pungent spice rub and cooked in stewed onions, roasted red peppers, and parsley. The chops pair beautifully with Simple Salad (page 134).

1 teaspoon extra-virgin olive oil

½ cup diced onion

½ cup diced roasted red pepper

2 tablespoons fresh parsley

½ cup red wine

⅛ teaspoon sea salt

Freshly ground black pepper

1 teaspoon minced garlic

½ teaspoon minced fresh rosemary

1 teaspoon smoked paprika

2 bone-in lamb shoulders, trimmed of fat

2 red potatoes, unpeeled, quartered

1. Grease the inside of the slow cooker with the olive oil.

2. Put the onion, red pepper, parsley, and wine into the slow cooker.

3. In a small bowl, combine the salt, a few grinds of the black pepper, garlic, rosemary, and paprika. Rub this mixture over the lamb chops. For even better flavor, do this one day ahead to allow all the flavors of the rub to permeate the meat. Place the chops into the slow cooker on top of the onion and wine mixture. The chops may need to slightly overlap one another to fit.

4. Place the potatoes on top of the lamb.

5. Cover and cook on low for 8 hours.

COOKING TIP Lamb often contains more fat than beef. To minimize the fat content of the finished recipe, trim all visible fat from the lamb and sear it in a hot skillet for 2 minutes on each side to render some of the fat and improve the flavor of the finished dish.

Korean-Style Short Ribs & Carrots

Serves 2

PREP
10 minutes

COOK
8 hours

PER SERVING
Calories: 532
Saturated Fat: 18g
Trans Fat: 0g
Carbohydrates: 15g
Fiber: 3g
Sodium: 1293mg
Protein: 18g

Serve these succulent short ribs with Chilled Rice Noodle Salad (page 142) or Orange-Soy Kale Salad with Mushrooms (page 138). Short ribs are nutrient dense, so the portion size is slightly less than in other meat recipes.

1 tablespoon low-sodium soy sauce

1 tablespoon fish sauce

1 tablespoon rice wine vinegar

1 teaspoon Sriracha

1 teaspoon toasted sesame oil

1 teaspoon minced garlic

1 teaspoon minced fresh ginger

8 ounces short ribs, trimmed of fat

4 carrots, cut into 2-inch pieces

2 cups low-sodium beef broth

1 scallion, white and green parts, sliced thin, for garnish

1. In a small bowl, whisk together the soy sauce, fish sauce, vinegar, Sriracha, sesame oil, garlic, and ginger. Spread this mixture onto the short ribs to coat thoroughly. You can do this one day ahead if you wish and keep the short ribs in the refrigerator.

2. Put the carrots into the slow cooker and then set the short ribs on top. Pour in the beef broth.

3. Cover and cook on low for 8 hours. To serve, garnish the short ribs with the scallions.

COOKING TIP Beef short ribs are a very rich cut of meat. Make sure to trim visible fat from the meat, which will reduce the fat content significantly without sacrificing flavor.

HEART
HEALTHY

DIABETES
FRIENDLY

ALLERGY
FRIENDLY

GLUTEN-
FREE

LOW
CALORIE

PREP
10 minutes

COOK
8 hours

PER SERVING
Calories: 526
Saturated Fat: 5g
Trans Fat: 0g
Carbohydrates: 10g
Fiber: 2g
Sodium: 576mg
Protein: 74g

Osso Buco

Serves 2

The slow cooker is the perfect vessel to cook osso buco. If you cannot find veal shanks or prefer not to eat veal, you can also use lamb or beef shanks for this recipe. It's an awesome meal for a special occasion or when you're craving something really rich. If you have the time, sear the veal in a hot skillet with a little extra-virgin olive oil, about 2 minutes per side, before placing it in the slow cooker.

1 teaspoon fresh rosemary

1 teaspoon fresh thyme

1 teaspoon minced garlic

½ tablespoon tomato paste

⅛ teaspoon sea salt

Freshly ground black pepper

1 veal shank, about 1 pound

½ cup diced onion

½ cup diced carrot

½ cup diced celery

½ teaspoon orange zest

½ cup dry red wine

1 cup low-sodium chicken or beef broth

1. In a small bowl, combine the rosemary, thyme, garlic, tomato paste, salt, and a few grinds of the black pepper. Coat the veal shank in this mixture. You can do this a day ahead if you wish and keep the veal in the refrigerator.

2. Put the onion, carrot, celery, orange zest, wine, and broth into the slow cooker. Stir thoroughly. Nestle the veal shank in the vegetable and wine mixture.

3. Cover and cook on low for 8 hours.

NUTRITION TIP Bone marrow is prized for its nutritional value. It is rich in minerals, protein, and collagen.

SUBSTITUTION TIP To ensure this dish is Allergy Friendly and Gluten-Free, use gluten-free low-sodium broth.

Adobo Steak Fajitas

— Serves 2 —

ALLERGY
FRIENDLY

GLUTEN-
FREE

Skirt steak is full of flavor, but sometimes isn't so tender. The slow cooker gives this cut a succulent texture, perfect for fajitas. This dish serves up nicely with Black Bean, Pepper & Corn Salad (page 143).

PREP
10 minutes

COOK
6 to 8 hours

1 tablespoon freshly squeezed lime juice

1 tablespoon minced garlic

2 tablespoons minced chipotles in adobo

1 tablespoon extra-virgin olive oil

⅛ teaspoon sea salt

12 ounces skirt steak, sliced thin

2 bell peppers, assorted colors, cored and cut into thin strips

½ onion, halved and cut into thin half circles

4 corn tortillas

1 small avocado, sliced, for garnish

PER SERVING
Calories: 791
Saturated Fat: 12g
Trans Fat: 0g
Carbohydrates: 46g
Fiber: 15g
Sodium: 501mg
Protein: 52g

1. In a small bowl, whisk together the lime juice, garlic, chipotles, olive oil, and salt. Add the skirt steak to the bowl and toss to thoroughly coat the meat. You can allow this to marinate overnight in the refrigerator if you wish.

2. Put the steak, peppers, and onions into the slow cooker.

3. Cover and cook on low for 6 to 8 hours. The vegetables and meat will be very tender.

4. Serve in warmed corn tortillas garnished with the avocado slices.

COOKING TIP Warm the tortillas in a dry skillet, or directly on a gas stovetop flame over low heat. Use tongs to turn each tortilla, heating for a few seconds on each side until warm and pliable. They can also be warmed in the microwave, for 10 seconds each.

SUBSTITUTION TIP Make sure to read the label of the chipotles in adobo. Sometimes the sauce contains potential allergens, including wheat flour and soybean oil.

HEART
HEALTHY

DIABETES
FRIENDLY

ALLERGY
FRIENDLY

LOW
CALORIE

PREP
10 minutes

COOK
8 hours

PER SERVING
Calories: 423
Saturated Fat: 5g
Trans Fat: 0g
Carbohydrates: 22g
Fiber: 2g
Sodium: 454mg
Protein: 51g

Irish-Style Lamb Stew

Serves 2

My great-grandmother immigrated to the United States from Ireland in the early 1900s, and St. Patrick's Day was always celebrated among our extended family. The main dish was corned beef and cabbage, flavors that were far too strong for my immature palate. This stew is a pleasing option for the holiday or any cool spring day that diners young and old will enjoy. Serve with Fluffy Buttermilk Biscuits (page 146) to sop up every last bite.

12 ounces boneless lamb shoulder or stew meat, cut into 1-inch pieces

⅛ teaspoon sea salt

Freshly ground black pepper

1 cup diced and peeled parsnips

1 cup diced and peeled potatoes

½ cup diced onions

1 tablespoon minced garlic

1 cup low-sodium beef broth

½ cup dark beer, such as Guinness Stout

½ tablespoon tomato paste

1. Season the lamb with the salt and a few grinds of the black pepper. Put the lamb, parsnips, potatoes, onions, and garlic into the slow cooker.

2. In a measuring cup or small bowl, whisk together the beef broth, beer, and tomato paste. Pour this over the lamb and vegetables.

3. Cover and cook on low for 8 hours.

VARIATION TIP Choose whatever root vegetables are in season and suit your taste. This stew also works well with turnips, rutabaga, and rainbow carrots.

SUBSTITUTION TIP To ensure this is Allergy Friendly, use gluten-free low-sodium beef broth.

Honey-Soy Lamb & Rice

Serves 2

GLUTEN-FREE

LOW CALORIE

PREP
10 minutes

COOK
8 hours

PER SERVING
Calories: 593
Saturated Fat: 5g
Trans Fat: 0g
Carbohydrates: 54g
Fiber: 2g
Sodium: 1049mg
Protein: 54g

Sweet, sour, salty, and oh-so-satisfying, this recipe allows the subtle flavors of the lamb to cut through the tangy marinade. Serve with Herbed Cucumbers (page 135).

1 teaspoon extra-virgin olive oil

½ cup brown rice

1 cup low-sodium chicken broth or water

1 scallion, white and green parts, sliced thin on a bias

2 tablespoons low-sodium soy sauce

2 tablespoons honey

1 tablespoon freshly squeezed lime juice

Pinch red pepper flakes

12 ounces boneless lamb shoulder, cut into 1-inch cubes

1. Grease the inside of the slow cooker with the olive oil.

2. Put the brown rice, broth, and scallion in the slow cooker. Stir to mix the ingredients and make sure the rice is submerged in the liquid.

3. In a large bowl, whisk together the soy sauce, honey, lime juice, and red pepper flakes. Add the lamb cubes and toss to coat them in this mixture. You can prepare the lamb a day ahead if you wish.

4. Place the lamb over the rice in the slow cooker.

5. Cover and cook on low for 8 hours.

COOKING TIP If you prefer the flavor of beef, use cubed beef chuck roast instead of lamb shoulder.

SUBSTITUTION TIP To ensure this dish is Gluten-Free, use gluten-free low-sodium chicken broth and soy sauce.

Seven

Grains & Pasta

122 Herbed Wild Rice,
     Bacon & Cherries

123 Lemon & Herb Barley Risotto

124 Wild Mushroom Risotto

125 Quinoa Ratatouille Casserole

126 Tex-Mex Quinoa

127 Gingery Quinoa Chicken

128 Wild Rice & Sweet Potatoes

129 Barley Primavera

130 Jalapeño-Bacon Mac & Cheese

131 Southwestern Rice Casserole

HEART
HEALTHY

DIABETES
FRIENDLY

ALLERGY
FRIENDLY

GLUTEN-
FREE

LOW
CALORIE

PREP
10 minutes

COOK
6 hours

PER SERVING
Calories: 350
Saturated Fat: 1g
Trans Fat: 0g
Carbohydrates: 66g
Fiber: 10g
Sodium: 268mg
Protein: 13g

Herbed Wild Rice, Bacon & Cherries

Serves 2

Applewood-smoked bacon adds a complexity of flavors and aromas to this dish. The bacon's warmth and smokiness is offset by the tart, sweet cherries and woody rosemary. For a complete meal, serve with two bone-in, skinless chicken breasts on top of the rice and season them with a second teaspoon of rosemary.

1 teaspoon extra-virgin olive oil

¾ cup wild rice

½ cup minced onion

1 piece applewood-smoked bacon, cooked and crumbled

1 teaspoon minced fresh rosemary

¼ cup dried cherries

2 cups low-sodium chicken broth

⅛ teaspoon sea salt

1. Grease the inside of the slow cooker with the olive oil.

2. Put all the ingredients into the slow cooker and stir them to mix thoroughly.

3. Cover and cook on low for 6 hours until the rice has absorbed all the water and is tender.

NUTRITION TIP For a vegan version of this dish, use low-sodium vegetable broth and swap the bacon for 2 tablespoons roughly chopped and toasted pecans. Stir in the pecans before serving the rice dish.

SUBSTITUTION TIP To ensure this is Allergy Friendly and Gluten-Free, use gluten-free low-sodium broth.

Lemon & Herb Barley Risotto

Serves 2

HEART
HEALTHY

DIABETES
FRIENDLY

LOW
CALORIE

———

PREP
10 minutes

COOK
6 to 8 hours

———

PER SERVING
Calories: 318
Saturated Fat: 1g
Trans Fat: 0g
Carbohydrates: 64g
Fiber: 13g
Sodium: 200mg
Protein: 10g

I absolutely love lemon season, but sometimes there are just so many of them, I don't know what to do with them all. Though they can be bought at most grocery stores, I finally made and tried preserved lemons and fell in love with their briny, bright complexity. They're perfect in this risotto paired with fresh herbs.

1 teaspoon extra-virgin olive oil

½ cup minced onion

2 tablespoons minced preserved lemon

1 teaspoon fresh thyme leaves

¼ cup roughly chopped fresh parsley, divided

¾ cup pearl barley

2 cups low-sodium vegetable broth

⅛ teaspoon sea salt

Freshly ground black pepper

½ lemon cut, into wedges, for garnish

1. Grease the inside of the slow cooker with olive oil. Add the onion, preserved lemon, thyme, 2 tablespoons of the parsley, barley, and vegetable broth. Season with the salt and pepper, and stir thoroughly.

2. Cover and cook on low for 6 to 8 hours, until the barley is tender and all the liquid is absorbed. Garnish each serving with the remaining parsley and a lemon wedge.

COOKING TIP It's so simple to make your own preserved lemons. First, slice 4 whole lemons into quarters and stuff them into a sterilized glass jar. Add 1 cup kosher salt, 1 tablespoon coriander seeds, 1 teaspoon fennel seeds, and a pinch of red chili flakes. Pour in enough lemon juice until the lemons are completely submerged. Tightly seal a lid on the jar and allow to rest at room temperature for at least one week before using.

PREP
10 minutes

COOK
6 to 8 hours

PER SERVING
Calories: 479
Saturated Fat: 3g
Trans Fat: 0g
Carbohydrates: 84g
Fiber: 1g
Sodium: 1018mg
Protein: 17g

Wild Mushroom Risotto

Serves 2

Mushrooms are so flavorful, especially dried mushrooms. They're also a fine substitute for red meat, keeping you feeling full with far fewer calories and no fat.

1 ounce dried wild mushrooms

1 teaspoon extra-virgin olive oil

½ cup minced onion

1 cup diced button mushrooms

1 teaspoon fresh thyme

1 cup short-grain white rice

2 cups low-sodium chicken or vegetable broth

⅛ teaspoon sea salt

Freshly ground black pepper

2 tablespoons grated Parmesan cheese

2 tablespoons minced fresh parsley, for garnish

½ lemon, cut into wedges, for garnish

1. Soak the dried mushrooms in 1 cup of very hot water while you prepare the other ingredients.

2. While the mushrooms are soaking, grease the inside of the slow cooker with the olive oil. Add the onion, button mushrooms, thyme, rice, and broth. Season with the salt and pepper and stir everything to mix well.

3. Remove the soaked mushrooms from the hot water, roughly chop them, and add them to the slow cooker.

4. Cover and cook on low for 6 to 8 hours, until the rice is tender and all the liquid is absorbed. Just before serving, stir in the Parmesan cheese and garnish each serving with the fresh parsley and a lemon wedge.

COOKING TIP I like to pulse dried mushrooms in my spice grinder to make a fine powder, instead of rehydrating them. It adds an awesome umami flavor to risotto and soups.

SUBSTITUTION TIP To ensure this dish is Gluten-Free, use gluten-free low-sodium chicken broth or vegetable broth.

Quinoa Ratatouille Casserole

Serves 2

HEART
HEALTHY

DIABETES
FRIENDLY

ALLERGY
FRIENDLY

GLUTEN-
FREE

LOW
CALORIE

PREP
10 minutes

COOK
8 hours

PER SERVING
Calories: 381
Saturated Fat: 1g
Trans Fat: 0g
Carbohydrates: 64g
Fiber: 9g
Sodium: 214mg
Protein: 15g

Ratatouille is full of flavor, but it's not quite filling enough to call it a meal. This nutrient-rich version of the classic French dish boasts many of the bright flavors of Provence. The addition of quinoa, a decidedly nontraditional ingredient and wonderful source of protein, makes this casserole a satisfying repast.

1 teaspoon extra-virgin olive oil

1 cup diced eggplant

1 cup diced zucchini

½ teaspoon sea salt

1 (15-ounce) can whole plum tomatoes, undrained, hand-crushed

1 teaspoon minced garlic

½ cup minced onion

1 cup quinoa

1 teaspoon herbes de Provence

1½ cups low-sodium chicken or vegetable broth

1. Grease the inside of the slow cooker with the olive oil.

2. Put the eggplant and zucchini in a colander in the sink. Season them liberally with the salt and allow it to rest for 10 minutes, or up to 30 minutes if you have the time.

3. Put the tomatoes, garlic, onion, quinoa, herbes de Provence, and broth in the slow cooker.

4. Rinse the eggplant and zucchini under cool water and gently press any excess moisture from the salted vegetables before adding to them to the slow cooker. Mix everything thoroughly.

5. Cover and cook on low for 8 hours.

COOKING TIP For a deep, rich color, consider using red quinoa instead of the traditional pale yellow quinoa. It has a similar flavor and texture.

SUBSTITUTION TIP To ensure this casserole is Allergy Friendly and Gluten-Free, use gluten-free low-sodium broth.

HEART
HEALTHY

DIABETES
FRIENDLY

ALLERGY
FRIENDLY

GLUTEN-
FREE

LOW
CALORIE

PREP
10 minutes

COOK
8 hours

PER SERVING
Calories: 453
Saturated Fat: 1g
Trans Fat: 0g
Carbohydrates: 82g
Fiber: 12g
Sodium: 418mg
Protein: 18g

Tex-Mex Quinoa

Serves 2

The zesty flavors in this vegan dish are so enjoyable you won't miss the meat. Then again, if you want a little more protein, add chicken tenderloins to the mix. Jalapeño peppers are milder than serrano and other varieties, so unless you like it really hot, stick with jalapeños.

1 cup quinoa, rinsed

2 cups low-sodium vegetable broth

½ cup minced onion

1 teaspoon minced garlic

½ cup corn kernels

½ cup black beans, drained and rinsed

½ cup canned fire-roasted diced tomatoes, undrained

½ jalapeño pepper, seeded and minced

1 teaspoon ground cumin

½ teaspoon smoked paprika

⅛ teaspoon sea salt

1. Put all the ingredients into the slow cooker and stir everything to mix thoroughly.

2. Cover and cook on low for 8 hours.

COOKING TIP Many recipes call for rinsing the quinoa before cooking it. This removes the saponins, which cover the quinoa grains and can upset stomachs. Unless you buy pre-rinsed quinoa, rinse the quinoa first.

SUBSTITUTION TIP To ensure this is Allergy Friendly and Gluten-Free, use gluten-free low-sodium broth.

Gingery Quinoa Chicken

Serves 2

HEART HEALTHY

DIABETES FRIENDLY

ALLERGY FRIENDLY

GLUTEN-FREE

LOW CALORIE

This dish is inspired by a recipe created by Tyler Florence in his cookbook *Tyler's Ultimate* and is one of my kids' favorites. The original recipe includes thawed frozen peas and fresh mint served on top of the finished dish, which work well with this recipe, too, if you wish to add them.

1 teaspoon extra-virgin olive oil

½ cup quinoa

½ cup low-sodium chicken broth

½ cup coconut milk

1 teaspoon minced fresh ginger

1 teaspoon minced garlic

Zest of 1 lime

½ teaspoon ground coriander

2 bone-in, skinless chicken thighs

⅛ teaspoon sea salt

Freshly ground black pepper

Juice of 1 lime, for garnish

1. Grease the inside of the slow cooker with the olive oil.

2. Put the quinoa, broth, coconut milk, ginger, garlic, zest, and coriander in the crock. Stir thoroughly.

3. Season the chicken thighs with the salt and a few grinds of the black pepper. Place them on top of the quinoa.

4. Cover and cook for 6 to 8 hours, until the quinoa has absorbed all the liquid and the chicken is cooked through.

5. Drizzle each portion with lime juice just before serving.

COOKING TIP Store fresh ginger in a basket on the kitchen counter uncovered. It lasts much longer at room temperature than when stored in the produce bin of the refrigerator.

SUBSTITUTION TIP To ensure this is Allergy Friendly and Gluten-Free, use gluten-free low-sodium chicken broth.

PREP
10 minutes

COOK
6 to 8 hours

PER SERVING
Calories: 545
Saturated Fat: 17g
Trans Fat: 0g
Carbohydrates: 33g
Fiber: 5g
Sodium: 384mg
Protein: 27g

HEART
HEALTHY

DIABETES
FRIENDLY

ALLERGY
FRIENDLY

GLUTEN-
FREE

LOW
CALORIE

PREP
10 minutes

COOK
6 to 8 hours

PER SERVING
Calories: 298
Saturated Fat: 1g
Trans Fat: 0g
Carbohydrates: 61g
Fiber: 7g
Sodium: 223mg
Protein: 12g

Wild Rice & Sweet Potatoes

Serves 2

The combined flavors and texture of cranberries, celery, onion, and sage will likely make you think of turkey dressing at Thanksgiving. Instead of bread crumbs, nutrient-rich wild rice and sweet potato are the basis of this healthy side dish. You can make it a complete meal by adding two bone-in chicken thighs to the top of the rice and sweet potatoes before cooking.

1 teaspoon extra-virgin olive oil

¾ cup wild rice

1 medium sweet potato, peeled and cut into 1-inch pieces

¼ cup minced celery

¼ cup minced onion

¼ cup dried cranberries

1 teaspoon minced fresh sage

1 teaspoon minced fresh thyme

2 cups low-sodium chicken broth

⅛ teaspoon sea salt

1. Grease the inside of the slow cooker with the olive oil.

2. Put all the ingredients in the slow cooker and stir them to mix thoroughly.

3. Cover and cook on low for 6 to 8 hours until the rice has absorbed all the liquid and is tender.

NUTRITION TIP Wild rice is rich in protein and fiber. It is also a good source of iron, magnesium, and vitamin B_6.

SUBSTITUTION TIP To ensure this is Allergy Friendly and Gluten-Free, use gluten-free low-sodium chicken broth.

Barley Primavera

Serves 2

HEART
HEALTHY

DIABETES
FRIENDLY

LOW
CALORIE

This dish is reminiscent of spaghetti in marinara sauce. Pearl barley is used as the starch because it stands up to long, slow cooking better than pasta noodles do. It is also a much better source of protein, fiber, and micronutrients than pasta.

PREP
10 minutes

COOK
8 hours

PER SERVING
Calories: 361
Saturated Fat: 1g
Trans Fat: 0g
Carbohydrates: 73g
Fiber: 16g
Sodium: 222mg
Protein: 12g

1 teaspoon extra-virgin olive oil

½ cup minced onion

½ cup diced carrot

1 cup diced zucchini

1 cup diced red bell pepper

1 teaspoon minced garlic

1 (15-ounce) can whole plum tomatoes, undrained, hand-crushed

2 tablespoons tomato paste

1 tablespoon Italian herbs

¾ cup pearl barley

1½ cups low-sodium chicken or vegetable broth

⅛ teaspoon sea salt

½ cup roughly chopped fresh basil, for garnish

1. Grease the inside of the slow cooker with the olive oil.

2. Put the onion, carrot, zucchini, bell pepper, garlic, tomatoes, tomato paste, Italian herbs, barley, broth, and salt in the slow cooker, and mix thoroughly.

3. Cover and cook on low for 8 hours, until the barley is tender and all the liquid is absorbed.

4. Garnish each serving with the fresh basil.

COOKING TIP Most tomato paste is sold in 6-ounce cans, resulting in waste if you don't use it all in one recipe or before it spoils. Consider purchasing a tube of tomato paste to keep in the refrigerator for use in multiple recipes. You may also freeze unused tomato paste in a zip-top bag.

PREP
10 minutes

COOK
6 hours

PER SERVING
Calories: 476
Saturated Fat: 9g
Trans Fat: 0g
Carbohydrates: 53g
Fiber: 5g
Sodium: 395mg
Protein: 25g

Jalapeño-Bacon Mac & Cheese

Serves 2

This recipe might not sound healthy, but it's loaded with protein and fiber and incorporates just enough of "the good stuff" to make it taste great. To beef up the healthy side of your meal, consider serving this dish with Simple Salad (page 134). You can find cooked bacon near other cured meats at the grocery store, or set aside a cooked strip of bacon from your morning breakfast.

1 teaspoon butter, at room temperature

½ cup fat-free evaporated milk

½ cup 2% milk

1 egg

½ cup sharp Cheddar cheese, grated

4 ounces whole-wheat elbow macaroni, cooked

1 strip bacon, cooked and crumbled

¼ cup canned jalapeño peppers

1. Grease the inside of the slow cooker with the butter.

2. In a large bowl, whisk together the evaporated milk, 2% milk, egg, and cheese.

3. Add the macaroni, bacon, and peppers to the bowl, and stir until thoroughly combined.

4. Pour the mixture into the slow cooker.

5. Cover and cook on low for 6 hours.

COOKING TIP Save time by preparing the macaroni the night before. Cook them until they are almost al dente and then drain and refrigerate until ready to use.

Southwestern Rice Casserole

Serves 2

HEART HEALTHY

GLUTEN-FREE

LOW CALORIE

PREP
10 minutes

COOK
4 to 6 hours

PER SERVING
Calories: 540
Saturated Fat: 4g
Trans Fat: 0g
Carbohydrates: 97g
Fiber: 13g
Sodium: 331mg
Protein: 25g

This vegetarian main dish is brimming with flavors of the Southwest. Make sure to wait until after the casserole is finished cooking to stir in the cheese and cilantro.

1 teaspoon extra-virgin olive oil

1 cup brown rice

1 cup canned black beans, drained and rinsed

1 cup frozen corn, thawed

1 cup canned fire-roasted diced tomatoes, undrained

1 teaspoon dried oregano

⅛ teaspoon cayenne pepper

⅛ teaspoon sea salt

1½ cups low-sodium vegetable broth or water

¼ cup fresh cilantro

¼ cup sharp cheddar cheese

1. Grease the inside of the slow cooker with the olive oil.

2. Add the brown rice, beans, corn, tomatoes, oregano, cayenne, and salt. Pour in the broth and stir to mix thoroughly.

3. Cover and cook on low for 4 to 6 hours.

4. Stir in the cilantro and cheddar cheese before serving.

VARIATION TIP For a fun presentation, cook the casserole as indicated and use as a filling for 4 to 6 bell peppers, topping each pepper with the cheese. Roast in the oven at 350°F.

SUBSTITUTION TIP To ensure this dish is Gluten-Free, use gluten-free vegetable broth.

eight

Quick & Easy Sides

134 Simple Salad

135 Herbed Cucumbers

136 Spinach Salad with
Figs & Walnuts

137 Cherry, Apple & Kale Salad

138 Orange-Soy Kale Salad
with Mushrooms

139 Blanched Green Bean Salad

140 Cilantro Rice Pilaf

141 Mediterranean Couscous

142 Chilled Rice Noodle Salad

143 Black Bean, Pepper &
Corn Salad

144 Black-Eyed Peas
with Rosemary

145 Whole-Grain Dinner Rolls

146 Fluffy Buttermilk Biscuits

147 Corn Bread

HEART
HEALTHY

DIABETES
FRIENDLY

ALLERGY
FRIENDLY

GLUTEN-
FREE

LOW
CALORIE

PREP
10 minutes

PER SERVING
Calories: 244
Saturated Fat: 2g
Trans Fat: 0g
Carbohydrates: 27g
Fiber: 8g
Sodium: 210mg
Protein: 7g

Simple Salad

Serves 2

Once you get the hang of making your own salad dressing, you may never go back to the bottled stuff again. You can whip up a variety of dressings in about two minutes and without any additives, preservatives, or allergens.

FOR THE DRESSING

1 tablespoon minced shallot

1 teaspoon fresh herbs, such as parsley, basil, or thyme

1 tablespoon white wine vinegar

Pinch sea salt

Freshly ground black pepper

2 tablespoons extra-virgin olive oil

FOR THE SALAD

4 cups fresh salad greens

2 small plum tomatoes, seeded and diced

1 cup peeled, diced cucumber

TO MAKE THE DRESSING

In a small glass jar, add the shallot, herbs, and vinegar and season it with the salt and pepper. Slowly drizzle in the olive oil, whisking constantly until emulsified.

TO MAKE THE SALAD

Put the salad greens, tomatoes, and cucumber in a large serving bowl. Drizzle the dressing over the top, and toss the salad to coat thoroughly.

COOKING TIP The basic formula for salad dressing is 1 tablespoon vinegar to 2 tablespoons oil. This ratio makes it easy to emulsify. Both honey and Dijon mustard act as emulsifiers, so if you want to use less oil in this recipe, add ½ teaspoon of either honey or mustard, and only whisk in as much oil as needed to fully blend.

Herbed Cucumbers

Serves 2

This refreshing little salad is delicious served with Spicy Mediterranean Beef Stew with Pearl Barley (page 59). It is best enjoyed immediately, and the ingredients are easy to assemble moments before the meal.

1 cucumber, peeled, seeded, and cut into ½-inch pieces

1 tablespoon fresh dill

1 tablespoon white wine vinegar

1 teaspoon extra-virgin olive oil

⅛ teaspoon sea salt

Freshly ground black pepper

1. Put the cucumber in a small serving bowl.

2. In a measuring cup, whisk together the dill, vinegar, olive oil, sea salt, and a few grinds of the black pepper.

3. Pour the dressing over the cucumbers and toss gently to mix. Serve immediately.

COOKING TIP If you purchase organic and unwaxed cucumber, leave it unpeeled. You'll get more nutrients and fiber.

PREP
5 minutes

PER SERVING
Calories: 48
Saturated Fat: 0g
Trans Fat: 0g
Carbohydrates: 6g
Fiber: 1g
Sodium: 124mg
Protein: 1g

HEART
HEALTHY

DIABETES
FRIENDLY

GLUTEN-
FREE

LOW
CALORIE

PREP
10 minutes

PER SERVING
Calories: 239
Saturated Fat: 2g
Trans Fat: 0g
Carbohydrates: 31g
Fiber: 6g
Sodium: 130mg
Protein: 5g

Spinach Salad with Figs & Walnuts

Serves 2

Fresh figs grow abundantly here in California. They are becoming more widely available around the country, but if you cannot find them, use dried figs and chop them into slivers to garnish this salad. The walnuts and sesame seeds add protein, healthy fat, and a delightful crunch, but both can be omitted if you're looking for an Allergy-Free dish.

2 tablespoons white wine vinegar

1 teaspoon honey

1 tablespoon extra-virgin olive oil

Sea salt

Freshly ground black pepper

4 cups fresh spinach, rinsed and hand torn

4 fresh figs, halved vertically

2 tablespoons toasted walnuts

1 teaspoon sesame seeds

1. In a large bowl, whisk together the vinegar and honey. Slowly drizzle in the olive oil, whisking constantly. Season the dressing with the salt and pepper.

2. Add the spinach to the dressing and toss gently to coat the leaves.

3. To serve, divide the spinach between serving plates. Garnish each with the figs, walnuts, and sesame seeds.

COOKING TIP The honey in this salad dressing helps emulsify the olive oil, so you can use less oil. However, if you prefer to leave it unsweetened, you may want to increase the olive oil for a homogenous dressing.

Cherry, Apple & Kale Salad

Serves 2

HEART
HEALTHY

DIABETES
FRIENDLY

ALLERGY
FRIENDLY

GLUTEN-
FREE

LOW
CALORIE

This kale salad recipe is popular in California. Traditionally made with dried cranberries, I use dried cherries instead for a healthier sweetness. You can easily make this side dish a complete meal by adding sliced cooked chicken and a sprinkle of pecans and feta cheese.

FOR THE DRESSING

1 tablespoon red wine vinegar

Pinch sea salt

Freshly ground black pepper

2 tablespoons extra-virgin olive oil

FOR THE SALAD

1 small bunch curly kale, ribs removed, roughly chopped

¼ cup dried cherries

1 apple, cored and julienned

PREP
10 minutes

PER SERVING
Calories: 305
Saturated Fat: 2g
Trans Fat: 0g
Carbohydrates: 43g
Fiber: 9g
Sodium: 179mg
Protein: 5g

TO MAKE THE DRESSING

Whisk together the vinegar, salt, and a few grinds of the black pepper in a large serving bowl. Slowly drizzle in the olive oil, whisking constantly.

TO MAKE THE SALAD

Add the kale, cherries, and apple to the bowl. Use your hands to thoroughly coat each of the leaves in the dressing. Serve immediately.

NUTRITION TIP Raw kale is loaded with powerful compounds that reduce your risk of cancer. It also has anti-inflammatory properties and helps your body's natural detoxification systems.

QUICK & EASY SIDES

HEART
HEALTHY

DIABETES
FRIENDLY

GLUTEN-
FREE

LOW
CALORIE

PREP
5 minutes

PER SERVING
Calories: 245
Saturated Fat: 2g
Trans Fat: 0g
Carbohydrates: 24g
Fiber: 2g
Sodium: 205mg
Protein: 9g

Orange-Soy Kale Salad with Mushrooms

Serves 2

There is a healthy counter service restaurant here in California called Lemonade that serves a kale salad with mushrooms and kumquats. I order it every time I visit! Here's my simple take on this sweet salad. The Lacinato kale used in this recipe is highly textured and slightly sweeter than green kale.

FOR THE DRESSING

½ teaspoon orange zest

1 tablespoon freshly squeezed orange juice

1 teaspoon low-sodium soy sauce

1 small shallot, minced

2 tablespoons extra-virgin olive oil

Freshly ground black pepper

FOR THE SALAD

1 cup quartered cremini mushrooms

1 bunch Lacinato kale, ribs removed

TO MAKE THE DRESSING

In a glass jar, whisk together the orange zest and juice, soy sauce, and shallots. Slowly drizzle in the olive oil, whisking constantly to emulsify the dressing. Season the dressing with a few grinds of the black pepper.

TO MAKE THE SALAD

1. Put the mushrooms in a large serving bowl. Pour the dressing over them, allowing them to soften slightly while you prepare the kale.

2. Cut the kale into very thin ribbons and add them to the bowl with the mushrooms. Use your hands to toss the kale with the dressing and mushrooms. Serve within 15 minutes.

COOKING TIP Save the kale ribs for juicing or add to homemade vegetable stock.

SUBSTITUTION TIP To ensure this dish is Gluten-Free, use gluten-free vegetable broth.

Blanched Green Bean Salad

Serves 4

The green beans can be prepared ahead of time and kept chilled until you're ready to serve this tangy salad. Store the cooled, blanched beans in a covered container in the refrigerator until you're ready to prepare the salad.

4 cups whole green beans, about 1 pound, stems removed

Sea salt

2 tablespoons prepared hummus

2 tablespoons freshly squeezed lemon juice

1 shallot, minced

1 plum tomato, diced

PREP
10 minutes

COOK
4 minutes

1. Over medium-high heat, bring a large pot of salted water to boil. Cook the green beans for about 4 minutes, until they are a bright green.

2. Meanwhile, prepare a large bowl of ice water.

3. Drain the green beans and immediately transfer them into the ice water. Allow the beans to cool completely before draining them again.

4. Arrange the blanched green beans in a serving bowl. In a small bowl, whisk together the hummus and lemon juice. Drizzle the sauce over the green beans. Top the salad with the shallot and tomato.

NUTRITION TIP This wonderful salad is loaded with antioxidants, vitamins, and healthy fat.

PER SERVING
Calories: 52
Saturated Fat: 0g
Trans Fat: 0g
Carbohydrates: 10g
Fiber: 4g
Sodium: 94mg
Protein: 3g

QUICK & EASY SIDES

HEART
HEALTHY

DIABETES
FRIENDLY

ALLERGY
FRIENDLY

GLUTEN-
FREE

LOW
CALORIE

PER SERVING
Calories: 174
Saturated Fat: 0g
Trans Fat: 0g
Carbohydrates: 36g
Fiber: 2g
Sodium: 67mg
Protein: 4g

Cilantro Rice Pilaf

Serves 4

Make this rice pilaf ahead of time and serve it as a side dish with an array of strongly flavored dishes. It is actually quite delicious served chilled, but you can warm it up if you wish. The recipe serves four to allow for leftovers that can be used for multiple meals.

1 cup long-grain brown rice

2 cups water

⅛ teaspoon sea salt

1 cup roughly chopped fresh cilantro

1 scallion, white and green parts, thinly sliced on the bias

Freshly ground black pepper

1. Add the rice, water, and salt to a small saucepan and heat over medium-high heat. Bring the water to a boil.

2. Reduce the heat to low, cover, and cook for 45 minutes, or until all the liquid is absorbed and the rice is tender.

3. Remove the pan from the heat. Fluff the rice with a fork, then stir in the cilantro and scallions. Season the rice with a few grinds of the black pepper, or to taste.

4. Serve warm, at room temperature, or chilled. Store leftovers in a covered container for up to 2 days in the refrigerator.

SUBSTITUTION TIP Brown rice is typically considered healthier and more nutrient-dense than white rice. Some people, however, find that white rice is more easily digestible. To use long-grain white rice, reduce the cooking time to about 20 minutes.

Mediterranean Couscous

Serves 4

Couscous looks like a grain, and is often mistaken for quinoa at first glance. It is really just bits of wheat pasta cut into tiny pieces. You can purchase regular or whole-grain couscous. Both cook in similar amounts of time. The whole grain has an almost imperceptibly grainier texture.

1 cup water

Pinch sea salt

1 cup couscous

¼ cup minced fresh parsley

1 cup diced plum tomatoes

1 shallot, minced

1 garlic clove, minced

¼ cup roughly chopped Kalamata olives

2 tablespoons extra-virgin olive oil

1 tablespoon red wine vinegar

1. In a small pot, bring the water and salt to a boil. Stir in the couscous. Cover the pot and remove it from the heat. Let it sit for 10 minutes.

2. Fluff the couscous with a fork then stir in the parsley, tomatoes, shallot, garlic, and olives.

3. In a small glass jar, whisk together the olive oil and vinegar.

4. Drizzle the dressing over the couscous. Stir the couscous until it is just combined with the dressing. Serve warm or at room temperature. Refrigerate leftovers in a covered container for up to 2 days.

SUBSTITUTION TIP Couscous is made with wheat and is therefore not gluten-free. This salad works just as well with cooked and cooled quinoa.

HEART HEALTHY

DIABETES FRIENDLY

LOW CALORIE

PREP
5 minutes

COOK
12 minutes

PER SERVING
Calories: 255
Saturated Fat: 1g
Trans Fat: 0g
Carbohydrates: 37g
Fiber: 3g
Sodium: 253mg
Protein: 7g

HEART
HEALTHY

DIABETES
FRIENDLY

GLUTEN-
FREE

LOW
CALORIE

PREP
15 minutes

PER SERVING
Calories: 96
Saturated Fat: 0g
Trans Fat: 0g
Carbohydrates: 18g
Fiber: 1g
Sodium: 50mg
Protein: 1g

Chilled Rice Noodle Salad

Serves 6

This easy chilled noodle salad works well with Korean-Style Short Ribs & Carrots (page 115) for a filling meal. You can find rice noodles in the international section of most grocery stores.

4 ounces thin rice noodles

2 cups water, very hot

Juice of 1 lime

½ teaspoon grated fresh ginger

½ teaspoon minced garlic

1 teaspoon honey

1 teaspoon low-sodium soy sauce

1 tablespoon toasted sesame oil

2 scallions, white and green parts, sliced thin on the bias

1. In a medium bowl, soak the rice noodles in the hot water for about 10 minutes until soft and pliable. Drain thoroughly.

2. In a large bowl, whisk together the lime juice, ginger, garlic, honey, and soy sauce. Drizzle in the sesame oil, whisking constantly.

3. Add the drained rice noodles and the scallions to the large bowl and use your hands or a pair of tongs to coat the noodles in the dressing.

4. Serve immediately or cover and chill. Refrigerate leftovers in a covered container for up to 3 days.

COOKING TIP You can use wider rice noodles, but they will take a few minutes longer to soak and soften.

SUBSTITUTION TIP To ensure this dish is Gluten-Free, use gluten-free low-sodium soy sauce.

Black Bean, Pepper & Corn Salad

Serves 4

This is one of my favorites to bring to potlucks and barbecues. Enjoy this salad chilled or at room temperature.

1 (15-ounce) can black beans, drained and rinsed

2 roasted whole red peppers, drained and diced

1 cup frozen roasted corn kernels, thawed

1 tablespoon freshly squeezed lime juice

1 tablespoon extra-virgin olive oil

1 teaspoon minced garlic

1 teaspoon ground cumin

1 teaspoon ground paprika

2 scallions, white and green parts, sliced thin on the bias

¼ cup minced fresh cilantro

Sea salt

Freshly ground black pepper

Put all the ingredients in a medium bowl and toss to combine. Season with the salt and black pepper.

SUBSTITUTION TIP If you cannot find roasted red peppers at your local supermarket, use a fresh red bell pepper instead. Just core it, removing the seeds and membrane before dicing.

HEART HEALTHY

DIABETES FRIENDLY

ALLERGY FRIENDLY

GLUTEN-FREE

LOW CALORIE

PREP
5 minutes

PER SERVING
Calories: 87
Saturated Fat: 1g
Trans Fat: 0g
Carbohydrates: 13g
Fiber: 2g
Sodium: 91mg
Protein: 3g

HEART
HEALTHY

DIABETES
FRIENDLY

ALLERGY
FRIENDLY

GLUTEN-
FREE

LOW
CALORIE

PREP
5 minutes

PER SERVING
Calories: 142
Saturated Fat: 1g
Trans Fat: 0g
Carbohydrates: 15g
Fiber: 4g
Sodium: 81mg
Protein: 5g

Black-Eyed Peas with Rosemary

Serves 4

This side dish is rich in protein, complex carbohydrates, and healthy fats. If you aren't a fan of rosemary, substitute another herb, such as thyme, basil, or sage, in place of the rosemary.

1 teaspoon minced fresh rosemary

1 teaspoon minced garlic

2 tablespoons red wine vinegar

⅛ teaspoon sea salt

Freshly ground black pepper

2 tablespoons extra-virgin olive oil

1 (15-ounce) can black-eyed peas, drained and rinsed

1. In a small serving bowl, whisk together the rosemary, garlic, vinegar, sea salt, and a few grinds of the black pepper. Slowly drizzle in the olive oil, whisking constantly.

2. Add the black-eyed peas to the bowl and stir gently to coat them in the dressing.

3. Serve immediately, or chill for several hours to allow the flavors to come together. Store in a covered container in the refrigerator for up to 3 days.

COOKING TIP If you prefer using dry black-eyed peas rather than canned, cook the dry peas in unsalted water for 20 minutes, or until tender. Drain and rinse under cool running water. Add the warm beans to the dressing. The warmth from the beans brings the all the flavors together nicely.

Whole-Grain Dinner Rolls

HEART
HEALTHY

DIABETES
FRIENDLY

LOW
CALORIE

Serves 12

These fiber-rich, whole-grain rolls are a cinch to prepare but they do take some time. Just whip up a batch on the weekend and store the unbaked dough in the freezer to bake them as needed. Allow the dough to cold-rise in the refrigerator during the day, and then pop in the oven for a fresh-baked delight.

2¼ cups whole-wheat pastry flour

1 tablespoon maple syrup or brown sugar

1 package active dry yeast

1 cup water, warmed to 110°F

3 tablespoons extra-virgin olive oil

1 egg, beaten

PREP
10 minutes,
plus 1 hour inactive
prep time

COOK
15 to 20 minutes

PER SERVING
Calories: 124
Saturated Fat: 1g
Trans Fat: 0g
Carbohydrates: 18g
Fiber: 2g
Sodium: 6mg
Protein: 3g

1. In a large bowl, mix all the ingredients together until just combined. Scrape down the sides of the bowl with a spatula.

2. Loosely cover the bowl with a light hand towel and set the bowl aside in a warm place for 1 hour to allow the dough to rise, or until it is just about doubled in volume.

3. While the dough is rising, line a 12-cup muffin tin with paper cups.

4. Once the dough is just about double in volume, punch it down and then spoon equal portions into each muffin cup. Put the tin into the freezer and allow the dough to freeze completely before transferring the dough portions, in their paper cups, to a sealed container.

5. When you want to bake the rolls, put the frozen dough portions in a muffin tin and put the tin in the refrigerator, allowing the dough to rise all day. Remove the tin with the dough from the refrigerator while you preheat the oven to 400°F. Bake the rolls for 15 to 20 minutes.

COOKING TIP If you prefer to bake some or all of the rolls right away, prepare the recipe through step 2. Then divide the dough into a muffin tin greased with cooking spray and allow the rolls to rise at room temperature for another hour. Bake in a 400°F oven for 15 to 20 minutes. Store the baked rolls in a covered container in the refrigerator or freezer.

PREP
5 minutes

COOK
12 to 14 minutes

PER SERVING
Calories: 182
Saturated Fat: 4g
Trans Fat: 0g
Carbohydrates: 27g
Fiber: 1g
Sodium: 144mg
Protein: 4g

Fluffy Buttermilk Biscuits

Serves 8

Whole-wheat pastry flour transformed the mealy bran muffins I had been making into a delicate, light, fluffy treat. I couldn't even tell they were made with whole-wheat flour. I've used both all-purpose flour and whole-wheat pastry flour in this recipe, but if you prefer a completely whole-grain biscuit, you can use whole-wheat pastry flour exclusively.

1 cup whole-wheat pastry flour

1 cup all-purpose flour, plus more for dusting

2½ teaspoons baking powder

½ teaspoon sea salt

4 tablespoons butter, cold, diced

¾ cup low-fat buttermilk

1 tablespoon maple syrup

1. Preheat the oven to 400°F. Line a baking sheet with parchment paper.

2. Combine the whole-wheat pastry flour, all-purpose flour, baking powder, and salt in a food processor. Pulse the mixture a few times to mix the ingredients together. Add the cold butter, and pulse until the mixture resembles coarse sand.

3. Add the buttermilk and maple syrup to the food processor and pulse everything until just combined.

4. Dust a clean work surface with some all-purpose flour. Scrape the dough from the food processor onto the floured surface and roll out the dough to about 1-inch thickness. Use a biscuit cutter or a clean round glass to cut out the biscuits. Place them on the baking sheet. Re-roll the leftover dough until you have biscuits or until it is all used up.

5. Bake for 12 to 14 minutes, or until puffed and lightly browned. Allow the biscuits to cool for a few minutes before serving.

6. Store leftovers in a covered container in a dry place for up to 4 days.

COOKING TIP If you follow a gluten-free diet, choose a gluten-free flour blend that you can use measure for measure in this recipe. The brand Cup4Cup is best in this recipe, but you can also use another brand or make your own. Just don't use one single flour as a replacement—a blend is essential to mimic the properties of wheat and for the biscuits to have a similar texture.

Corn Bread

HEART
HEALTHY

DIABETES
FRIENDLY

LOW
CALORIE

Mix the dry ingredients together ahead of time and store in a mason jar so that you're ready to bake this delicious corn bread in the oven at a moment's notice.

1 teaspoon unsalted butter, at room temperature

1 cup stone-ground cornmeal

¾ cup whole-wheat pastry flour

1½ teaspoons baking powder

½ teaspoon baking soda

⅛ teaspoon sea salt

½ cup applesauce

2 eggs, beaten

1½ cups plain yogurt

PREP
5 minutes

COOK
25 minutes

PER SERVING
Calories: 158
Saturated Fat: 1g
Trans Fat: 0g
Carbohydrates: 26g
Fiber: 2g
Sodium: 168mg
Protein: 7g

1. Preheat the oven to 400°F.

2. Grease the inside of an 8-by-8-inch baking dish with the butter.

3. Put the cornmeal, flour, baking powder, baking soda, and salt in a medium bowl and stir to combine.

4. Whisk in the applesauce, eggs, and yogurt until just combined. Pour the mixture into the prepared pan.

5. Bake for 20 to 25 minutes, until a toothpick inserted in the center comes out clean.

SUBSTITUTION TIP If you don't have yogurt on hand, use 1 tablespoon lemon juice added to 1½ cups low-fat milk instead.

Measurement Conversions

Volume Equivalents (Liquid)

U.S. STANDARD	U.S. STANDARD (OUNCES)	METRIC (APPROXIMATE)
2 tablespoons	1 fl. oz.	30 mL
¼ cup	2 fl. oz.	60 mL
½ cup	4 fl. oz.	120 mL
1 cup	8 fl. oz.	240 mL
1½ cups	12 fl. oz.	355 mL
2 cups or 1 pint	16 fl. oz.	475 mL
4 cups or 1 quart	32 fl. oz.	1 L
1 gallon	128 fl. oz.	4 L

Oven Temperatures

FAHRENHEIT (F)	CELSIUS (C) (APPROXIMATE)
250°	120°
300°	150°
325°	165°
350°	180°
375°	190°
400°	200°
425°	220°
450°	230°

Volume Equivalents (Dry)

U.S. STANDARD	METRIC (APPROXIMATE)
⅛ teaspoon	0.5 mL
¼ teaspoon	1 mL
½ teaspoon	2 mL
¾ teaspoon	4 mL
1 teaspoon	5 mL
1 tablespoon	15 mL
¼ cup	59 mL
⅓ cup	79 mL
½ cup	118 mL
⅔ cup	156 mL
¾ cup	177 mL
1 cup	235 mL
2 cups or 1 pint	475 mL
3 cups	700 mL
4 cups or 1 quart	1 L

Weight Equivalents

U.S. STANDARD	METRIC (APPROXIMATE)
½ ounce	15 g
1 ounce	30 g
2 ounces	60 g
4 ounces	115 g
8 ounces	225 g
12 ounces	340 g
16 ounces or 1 pound	455 g

The Dirty Dozen & The Clean Fifteen

A nonprofit environmental watchdog organization called Environmental Working Group (EWG) looks at data supplied by the US Department of Agriculture (USDA) and the Food and Drug Administration (FDA) about pesticide residues. Each year it compiles a list of the best and worst pesticide loads found in commercial crops. You can use these lists to decide which fruits and vegetables to buy organic to minimize your exposure to pesticides and which produce is considered safe enough to buy conventionally. This does not mean they are pesticide-free, though, so wash these fruits and vegetables thoroughly.

These lists change every year, so make sure you look up the most recent one before you fill your shopping cart. You'll find the most recent lists as well as a guide to pesticides in produce at EWG.org/FoodNews.

Dirty Dozen

Apples
Celery
Cherry tomatoes
Cucumbers
Grapes
Nectarines (imported)

Peaches
Potatoes
Snap peas (imported)
Spinach
Strawberries
Sweet bell peppers

In addition to the Dirty Dozen, the EWG added two types of produce contaminated with highly toxic organo-phosphate insecticides:

Kale/Collard greens
Hot peppers

Clean Fifteen

Asparagus
Avocados
Cabbage
Cantaloupes (domestic)
Cauliflower

Eggplants
Grapefruits
Kiwis
Mangos
Onions

Papayas
Pineapples
Sweet corn
Sweet peas (frozen)
Sweet potatoes

References

Abbas, Abul K., Andrew H. Lichtman, and Shiv Pillai. *Basic Immunology: Functions and Disorders of the Immune System.* 4th ed. Philadelphia: Saunders, 2012.

American Heart Association. "The American Heart Association's Diet and Lifestyle Recommendations." Accessed October 8, 2015. www.heart.org/HEARTORG /GettingHealthy/NutritionCenter/HealthyEating/The-American-Heart -Associations-Diet-and-Lifestyle-Recommendations_UCM_305855_Article.jsp.

Florence, Tyler. *Tyler's Ultimate.* New York: Random House, 2006.

The Guardian. "Roundup Weedkiller 'Probably' Causes Cancer, Says WHO Study." Accessed October 21, 2015. www.theguardian.com/environment/2015/mar/21 /roundup-cancer-who-glyphosate-.

Khan, Alam, Mahpara Safdar, Mohammad Muzaffar Ali Kahn, Khan Nawaz Khattak, and Richard A. Anderson. "Cinnamon Improves Glucose and Lipids of People with Type 2 Diabetes." *Diabetes Care.* Accessed October 12, 2015. care.diabetesjournals.org/content/26/12/3215.full.

Mayo Clinic. "Diabetes Diet: Create Your Healthy Eating Plan." Accessed October 8, 2015. www.mayoclinic.org/diseases-conditions/diabetes/in-depth/diabetes-diet /art-20044295?pg=2.

Nevin, K.G., and T. Rajamohan. "Influence of Virgin Coconut Oil on Blood Coagulation Factors, Lipid Levels and LDL Oxisantion in Cholesterol Fed Sprague-Dawley Rats." *European e-Journal of Clinical Nutrition and Metabolism* 3, no. 1 (February 2008): e1–e8. doi: http://dx.doi.org/10.1016/j.eclnm.2007.09.003.

Pollan, Michael. *In Defense of Food: An Eater's Manifesto.* New York: Penguin Group, 2008.

Rothberg, Michael B., and Senthil K. Sivalingam. "The New Heart Failure Diet: Less Salt Restriction, More Micronutrients." *Journal of General Internal Medicine* 25, no 10 (October 2010): 1136-1137 Accessed October 12, 2015. www.ncbi.nlm.nih .gov/pmc/articles/PMC2955483/

United States Department of Agriculture. "Danger Zone." Accessed October 9, 2015. www.fsis.usda.gov/wps/portal/fsis/topics/food-safety-education/get-answers /food-safety-fact-sheets/safe-food-handling/danger-zone-40-f-140-f/CT_Index.

United States Department of Agriculture. "Slow Cookers and Food Safety." Accessed October 9, 2015. www.fsis.usda.gov/wps/portal/fsis/topics/food-safety- education/get-answers/food-safety-fact-sheets/appliances-and-thermometers /slow-cookers-and-food-safety/ct_index.

Uribarri, Jaime, et al. "Advanced Glycation End Products in Foods and a Practical Guide to Their Reduction in the Diet." *Journal of the American Dietetic Association*. June 2010. Accessed November 10, 2015. www.ncbi.nlm.nih.gov /pmc/articles/PMC3704564/

Wanjek, Christopher. "Dark Meat Can be Heart Healthy, Study Shows." Live Science. March 6, 2012. Accessed October 16, 2015. www.livescience.com/18848-dark -meat-heart-healthy.html.

Whole Foods Market. "Easy Whole Wheat Dinner Rolls." Accessed October 19, 2015. www.wholefoodsmarket.com/recipe/easy-whole-wheat-dinner-rolls.

The World's Healthiest Foods. "Swiss Chard." Accessed October 15, 2015. www.whfoods.com/genpage.php?tname=foodspice&dbid=16.

Recipe Index

A

Adobo Steak Fajitas, 117

B

Baked Potato Soup, 47

Balsamic-Glazed Beef with Red Cabbage, 110

Balsamic-Glazed Pork Tenderloin & Carrots, 96

Banana Nut French Toast, 28

Barbecue Kabocha Squash, 62

Barley Primavera, 129

Beef Barley Soup, 57

Beef Broccoli, 109

Beef Goulash with Pumpkin, Mushrooms & Pumpkin Seeds, 107

Beef Ragù, 111

Black Bean, Pepper & Corn Salad, 143

Black-Eyed Peas with Rosemary, 144

Blanched Green Bean Salad, 139

Braised Quinoa, Kale & Summer Squash, 63

Breakfast Quinoa & Fruit, 25

Butter Seitan & Chickpeas, 71

C

Carnitas with Avocado, Cilantro & Queso Fresco, 101

Cashew Chicken & Snap Peas, 92

Cassoulet, 91

Cherry, Apple & Kale Salad, 137

Cherry-Studded Quinoa Porridge, 26

Chicken & Artichoke Bake, 81

Chicken Chili Verde over Rice, 86

Chicken Fajitas, 89

Chicken Fajita Soup, 56

Chicken & Grape Tomatoes, 80

Chicken in Mango Chutney, 82

Chicken Noodle Soup, 54

Chicken Pot Pie, 85

Chicken Tikka Masala, 93

Chicken with Mushrooms & Shallots, 83

Chilled Rice Noodle Salad, 142

Chipotle Black Bean Soup, 49

Cilantro Rice Pilaf, 140

Cinnamon Raisin Steel-Cut Oatmeal, 22

Coq au Vin Blanc, 90

Corn Bread, 147

Corn & Potato Chowder, 51

Corn & Red Pepper Chowder, 45

Cranberry-Glazed PorkTenderloin, 100

Cream of Fennel & Leek Soup, 41

Creamy Butternut Squash & Parsnip Soup, 39

Cuban-Style Pork Street Tacos, 98

Curried Sweet Potatoes with Broccoli & Cashews, 66

F

Fluffy Buttermilk Biscuits, 146

G

Garlicky Chicken Kale Soup, 55

Ginger Carrot Bisque, 38

Gingery Quinoa Chicken, 127

Greek-Style Lamb Shoulder & Lemon Potatoes, 113

Ground Beef–Stuffed Bell Peppers, 106

H

Ham and Cheese Breakfast Casserole, 34

Herbed Cucumbers, 135

Herbed Wild Rice, Bacon & Cherries, 122

Honey-Soy Lamb & Rice, 119

I

Irish-Style Lamb Stew, 118

J

Jalapeño-Bacon Mac & Cheese, 130

K

Korean-Style Short Ribs & Carrots, 115

L

Lemon & Herb Barley Risotto, 123

Lentil, Chickpea & White Bean Stew, 58

M

Meatloaf, 105

Mediterranean Couscous, 141

Minestrone, 48

Mixed Bean Chili, 65

Moroccan-Style Chickpeas
    with Chard, 67

Mushroom Soup, 40

O

Orange-Soy Kale Salad with
    Mushrooms, 138

Osso Buco, 116

P

Pear Chai-Spiced Oatmeal, 23

Pesto Chicken with Stewed
    Vegetables, 84

Pork Chops with Apples
    & Onions, 94

Pork Chops with Mashed
    Sweet Potatoes, 99

Pork Tenderloin with
    Rosemary Peaches, 95

Pot Roast, 108

Prosciutto, Rosemary & Potato
    Breakfast Casserole, 33

Pumpkin Black Bean Chili, 53

Pumpkin Spice Oatmeal, 24

Q

Quinoa Ratatouille
    Casserole, 125

R

Red Curry Butternut
    Squash Soup, 50

Roasted Red Pepper &
    Mozzarella Stuffed
    Chicken Breasts, 88

Rosemary Cauliflower
    & Lentils, 64

Rosemary Parsnip Bisque
    with Toasted Bread
    Crumbs, 44

Rutabaga & Sweet Potato
    Soup with Garlicky
    Ground Walnuts, 46

S

Sausage, Fennel & Chicken, 87

Seitan Tikka Masala, 70

Shepherd's Pie, 104

Simple Salad, 134

Smoked Salmon & Potato
    Casserole, 32

Southwest Breakfast
    Casserole, 35

Southwestern Rice
    Casserole, 131

Southwest Sweet Potato &
    Corn Scramble, 31

Soy-Ginger Pork Chops with
    Green Beans, 97

Spanish-Style Lamb Chops, 114

Spiced Pot Roast with Celery
    & Mushrooms, 112

Spicy Peanut Rice Bake, 76

Spicy Mediterranean
    Beef Stew with
    Pearl Barley, 59

Spinach & Black Bean
    Enchilada Pie, 68

Spinach, Mushroom
    & Swiss Cheese
    Crustless Quiche, 69

Spinach Salad with Figs
    & Walnuts, 136

Split Pea Soup, 43

Strawberry Cream Cheese
    French Toast, 27

Sweet Spiced Lentil Soup, 42

T

Tempeh Shepherd's Pie, 72

Tempeh-Stuffed Bell
    Peppers, 73

Tex-Mex Quinoa, 126

Tofu Red Curry with
    Green Beans, 74

Tofu Stir-Fry, 75

V

Vegetable Curry Soup, 52

Vegetarian Cassoulet, 77

W

Whole-Grain Dinner Rolls, 145

Wild Mushroom Risotto, 124

Wild Rice & Sweet
    Potatoes, 128

Y

Yogurt & Berry Parfait, 30

Yogurt with Mangos &
    Cardamom, 29

Index

A

Adobo Steak Fajitas, 117
Allergy Friendly, 13
Almond milk
  Cherry-Studded Quinoa
    Porridge, 26
  Cinnamon Raisin
    Steel-Cut Oatmeal, 22
  Pear Chai-Spiced
    Oatmeal, 23
  Pumpkin Spice Oatmeal, 24
Apples
  Cherry, Apple &
    Kale Salad, 137
  Creamy Butternut Squash
    & Parsnip Soup, 39
  Pork Chops with Apples
    & Onions, 94
  Sweet Spiced Lentil
    Soup, 42
Artichoke, Chicken &, Bake, 81
Avocado
  Adobo Steak Fajitas, 117
  Carnitas with Avocado,
    Cilantro & Queso
    Fresco, 101
  Chicken Fajitas, 89
  Chipotle Black Bean
    Soup, 49

B

Bacon
  Baked Potato Soup, 47
  Cassoulet, 91
  Herbed Wild Rice, Bacon
    & Cherries, 122
  Jalapeño-Bacon Mac
    & Cheese, 130
Baked Potato Soup, 47
Balsamic-Glazed Beef with
  Red Cabbage, 110
Balsamic-Glazed Pork
    Tenderloin & Carrots, 96
Banana Nut French Toast, 28
Barbecue Kabocha Squash, 62
Barley
  Barley Primavera, 129
  Beef Barley Soup, 57
  Lemon & Herb Barley
    Risotto, 123
  Spicy Mediterranean
    Beef Stew with
    Pearl Barley, 59
Basil
  Barley Primavera, 129
  Chicken & Artichoke
    Bake, 81
  Roasted Red Pepper &
    Mozzarella Stuffed
    Chicken Breasts, 88
Beans. See also Black
    beans; Chickpeas;
    Green beans; Kidney
    beans; Navy beans
  Mixed Bean Chili, 65
Beef
  Adobo Steak Fajitas, 117
  Balsamic-Glazed Beef
    with Red Cabbage, 110
  Beef Barley Soup, 57
  Beef Broccoli, 109

  Beef Goulash with
    Pumpkin, Mushrooms
    & Pumpkin Seeds, 107
  Beef Ragù, 111
  Korean-Style Short
    Ribs & Carrots, 115
  Osso Buco, 116
  Pot Roast, 108
  Spiced Pot Roast with
    Celery & Mushrooms, 112
  Spicy Mediterranean
    Beef Stew with
    Pearl Barley, 59
Beef broth
  Beef Barley Soup, 57
  Beef Broccoli, 109
  Beef Ragù, 111
  Irish-Style Lamb Stew, 118
  Korean-Style Short
    Ribs & Carrots, 115
  Osso Buco, 116
  Pot Roast, 108
  Spiced Pot Roast with
    Celery & Mushrooms, 112
Beer
  Irish-Style Lamb Stew, 118
Belgian endives
  Cranberry-Glazed Pork
    Tenderloin, 100
Bell peppers. See also
    Green bell peppers;
    Red bell peppers
  Adobo Steak Fajitas, 117
  Chicken Fajitas, 89
Black beans
  Black Bean, Pepper &
    Corn Salad, 143

Chicken Fajita Soup, 56
Chipotle Black Bean
    Soup, 49
Pumpkin Black
    Bean Chili, 53
Southwest Breakfast
    Casserole, 35
Southwestern Rice
    Casserole, 131
Spinach & Black Bean
    Enchilada Pie, 68
Tex-Mex Quinoa, 126
Black-Eyed Peas with
    Rosemary, 144
Blanched Green Bean
    Salad, 139
Blueberries
    Yogurt & Berry Parfait, 30
Braised Quinoa, Kale &
    Summer Squash, 63
Breads
    Corn Bread, 147
    Fluffy Buttermilk
        Biscuits, 146
    Whole-Grain Dinner
        Rolls, 145
Breakfast and Brunch
    Banana Nut French
        Toast, 28
    Breakfast Quinoa
        & Fruit, 25
    Cherry-Studded Quinoa
        Porridge, 26
    Cinnamon Raisin
        Steel-Cut Oatmeal, 22
    Ham and Cheese Breakfast
        Casserole, 34

Pear Chai-Spiced
    Oatmeal, 23
Prosciutto, Rosemary
    & Potato Breakfast
    Casserole, 33
Pumpkin Spice Oatmeal, 24
Smoked Salmon &
    Potato Casserole, 32
Southwest Breakfast
    Casserole, 35
Southwest Sweet Potato
    & Corn Scramble, 31
Strawberry Cream Cheese
    French Toast, 27
Yogurt & Berry Parfait, 30
Yogurt with Mangos
    & Cardamom, 29
Broccoli
    Beef Broccoli, 109
    Curried Sweet Potatoes
        with Broccoli &
        Cashews, 66
Broth. See Beef broth; Chicken
    broth; Vegetable broth
Brown rice
    Chicken Chili Verde
        over Rice, 86
    Cilantro Rice Pilaf, 140
    Southwestern Rice
        Casserole, 131
    Spicy Peanut Rice Bake, 76
    Tofu Stir-Fry, 75
Bulk buying, 19
Buttermilk, Fluffy,
    Biscuits, 146

Butternut squash
    Beef Goulash with
        Pumpkin, Mushrooms
        & Pumpkin Seeds, 107
    Creamy Butternut Squash
        & Parsnip Soup, 39
    Red Curry Butternut
        Squash Soup, 50
Butter Seitan & Chickpeas, 71

C
Cabbage. See Red cabbage
Carnitas with Avocado,
    Cilantro & Queso
    Fresco, 101
Carrots
    Balsamic-Glazed Pork
        Tenderloin & Carrots, 96
    Chicken Noodle Soup, 54
    Chicken Pot Pie, 85
    Ginger Carrot Bisque, 38
    Korean-Style Short
        Ribs & Carrots, 115
    Minestrone, 48
    Pot Roast, 108
    Shepherd's Pie, 104
    Spiced Pot Roast with
        Celery & Mushrooms, 112
    Tempeh Shepherd's Pie, 72
    Tofu Stir-Fry, 75
Cashews
    Cashew Chicken &
        Snap Peas, 92
    Curried Sweet Potatoes
        with Broccoli &
        Cashews, 66
Cassoulet, 91

Cauliflower, Rosemary,
& Lentils, 64
Celery
Chicken Noodle Soup, 54
Spiced Pot Roast with
Celery & Mushrooms, 112
Cheddar cheese
Baked Potato Soup, 47
Chicken Fajita Soup, 56
Jalapeño-Bacon Mac
& Cheese, 130
Pumpkin Black
Bean Chili, 53
Shepherd's Pie, 104
Southwestern Rice
Casserole, 131
Tempeh Shepherd's Pie, 72
Cheese. *See* Cheddar cheese;
Mozzarella cheese;
Parmesan cheese;
Pepper Jack cheese;
Swiss cheese
Cherries
Cherry, Apple &
Kale Salad, 137
Cherry-Studded Quinoa
Porridge, 26
Herbed Wild Rice, Bacon
& Cherries, 122
Chicken
Cashew Chicken &
Snap Peas, 92
Cassoulet, 91
Chicken & Artichoke
Bake, 81
Chicken Chili Verde
over Rice, 86
Chicken Fajitas, 89
Chicken Fajita Soup, 56
Chicken & Grape
Tomatoes, 80
Chicken in Mango
Chutney, 82

Chicken Noodle Soup, 54
Chicken Pot Pie, 85
Chicken Tikka Masala, 93
Chicken with Mushrooms
& Shallots, 83
Coq au Vin Blanc, 90
Garlicky Chicken
Kale Soup, 55
Gingery Quinoa
Chicken, 127
Pesto Chicken with
Stewed Vegetables, 84
Roasted Red Pepper &
Mozzarella Stuffed
Chicken Breasts, 88
Sausage, Fennel &
Chicken, 87
Chicken broth
Baked Potato Soup, 47
Balsamic-Glazed Pork
Tenderloin & Carrots, 96
Barley Primavera, 129
Beef Goulash with
Pumpkin, Mushrooms
& Pumpkin Seeds, 107
Carnitas with Avocado,
Cilantro & Queso
Fresco, 101
Cassoulet, 91
Chicken Chili Verde
over Rice, 86
Chicken Fajita Soup, 56
Chicken Noodle Soup, 54
Chicken Pot Pie, 85
Chicken Tikka Masala, 93
Chipotle Black Bean
Soup, 49
Corn & Potato Chowder, 51
Corn & Red Pepper
Chowder, 45
Cranberry-Glazed Pork
Tenderloin, 100

Cream of Fennel &
Leek Soup, 41
Garlicky Chicken
Kale Soup, 55
Ginger Carrot Bisque, 38
Gingery Quinoa
Chicken, 127
Honey-Soy Lamb
& Rice, 119
Mushroom Soup, 40
Osso Buco, 116
Pork Chops with Mashed
Sweet Potatoes, 99
Quinoa Ratatouille
Casserole, 125
Red Curry Butternut
Squash Soup, 50
Rosemary Parsnip
Bisque with Toasted
Bread Crumbs, 44
Soy-Ginger Pork Chops
with Green Beans, 97
Split Pea Soup, 43
Sweet Spiced Lentil
Soup, 42
Vegetable Curry Soup, 52
Wild Mushroom
Risotto, 124
Wild Rice & Sweet
Potatoes, 128
Chickpeas
Braised Quinoa, Kale &
Summer Squash, 63
Butter Seitan &
Chickpeas, 71
Lentil, Chickpea & White
Bean Stew, 58
Moroccan-Style Chickpeas
with Chard, 67
Chili
Mixed Bean Chili, 65
Pumpkin Black
Bean Chili, 53

Chilled Rice Noodle Salad, 142
Chipotle Black Bean Soup, 49
Cilantro Rice Pilaf, 140
Cinnamon Raisin Steel-Cut
  Oatmeal, 22
Clean Fifteen, 150
Coconut milk
  Butter Seitan &
    Chickpeas, 71
  Curried Sweet Potatoes
    with Broccoli &
    Cashews, 66
  Gingery Quinoa
    Chicken, 127
  Tofu Red Curry with
    Green Beans, 74
  Vegetable Curry Soup, 52
Collard leaves
  Spicy Peanut Rice Bake, 76
Coq au Vin Blanc, 90
Corn
  Black Bean, Pepper &
    Corn Salad, 143
  Chicken Fajita Soup, 56
  Corn & Potato Chowder, 51
  Corn & Red Pepper
    Chowder, 45
  Mixed Bean Chili, 65
  Southwest Sweet Potato
    & Corn Scramble, 31
  Southwestern Rice
    Casserole, 131
  Tempeh-Stuffed Bell
    Peppers, 73
  Tex-Mex Quinoa, 126
Corn Bread, 147
Couscous, Mediterranean, 141
Cranberries
  Cranberry-Glazed Pork
    Tenderloin, 100
  Wild Rice & Sweet
    Potatoes, 128

Cream cheese, Strawberry,
  French Toast, 27
Cream of Fennel &
  Leek Soup, 41
Creamy Butternut Squash
  & Parsnip Soup, 39
Cuban-Style Pork Street
  Tacos, 98
Cucumbers
  Herbed Cucumbers, 135
  Simple Salad, 134
Curried Sweet Potatoes with
  Broccoli & Cashews, 66

D
Diabetes Friendly, 13
Dirty Dozen, 150

E
Egg noodles
  Chicken Noodle Soup, 54
Eggplant
  Quinoa Ratatouille
    Casserole, 125
  Vegetable Curry Soup, 52
Eggs
  Banana Nut French
    Toast, 28
  Ham & Cheese Breakfast
    Casserole, 34
  Prosciutto, Rosemary
    & Potato Breakfast
    Casserole, 33
  Smoked Salmon &
    Potato Casserole, 32
  Southwest Breakfast
    Casserole, 35
  Southwest Sweet Potato
    & Corn Scramble, 31
  Spinach, Mushroom
    & Swiss Cheese
    Crustless Quiche, 69

Strawberry Cream Cheese
  French Toast, 27
Egg whites
  Ham & Cheese Breakfast
    Casserole, 34
  Southwest Breakfast
    Casserole, 35
Elbow macaroni
  Jalapeño-Bacon Mac
    & Cheese, 130
Enchilada sauce
  Spinach & Black Bean
    Enchilada Pie, 68

F
Fajitas
  Adobo Steak Fajitas, 117
  Chicken Fajitas, 89
Fennel
  Cream of Fennel &
    Leek Soup, 41
  Sausage, Fennel &
    Chicken, 87
Figs, Spinach Salad with,
  & Walnuts, 136
Fire-roasted tomatoes
  Chicken Fajita Soup, 56
  Mixed Bean Chili, 65
  Pumpkin Black
    Bean Chili, 53
  Seitan Tikka Masala, 70
  Southwest Breakfast
    Casserole, 35
  Southwestern Rice
    Casserole, 131
  Tex-Mex Quinoa, 126
Fish and Seafood
  Smoked Salmon &
    Potato Casserole, 32
Fluffy Buttermilk Biscuits, 146

G

Garlicky Chicken Kale
    Soup, 55
Ginger
    Ginger Carrot Bisque, 38
    Gingery Quinoa
        Chicken, 127
Gluten-Free, 13
Grains & Pasta
    Barley Primavera, 129
    Chicken Noodle Soup, 54
    Gingery Quinoa
        Chicken, 127
    Herbed Wild Rice, Bacon
        & Cherries, 122
    Jalapeño-Bacon Mac
        & Cheese, 130
    Lemon & Herb Barley
        Risotto, 123
    Quinoa Ratatouille
        Casserole, 125
    Southwestern Rice
        Casserole, 131
    Tex-Mex Quinoa, 126
    Wild Mushroom
        Risotto, 124
    Wild Rice & Sweet
        Potatoes, 128
Grape tomatoes
    Chicken & Grape
        Tomatoes, 80
    Pesto Chicken with
        Stewed Vegetables, 84
Greek-Style Lamb Shoulder
    & Lemon Potatoes, 113
Green beans
    Blanched Green Bean
        Salad, 139
    Minestrone, 48
    Seitan Tikka Masala, 70
    Soy-Ginger Pork Chops
        with Green Beans, 97

Tofu Red Curry with
    Green Beans, 74
Tofu Stir-Fry, 75
Green bell peppers
    Cuban-Style Pork
        Street Tacos, 98
    Pumpkin Black
        Bean Chili, 53
    Tofu Stir-Fry, 75
Ground beef
    Ground Beef–Stuffed
        Bell Peppers, 106
    Meatloaf, 105
    Shepherd's Pie, 104

H

Ham. *See also* Prosciutto
    Ham & Cheese Breakfast
        Casserole, 34
Heart Healthy, 12–13
Heavy cream
    Ginger Carrot Bisque, 38
Herbed Cucumbers, 135
Herbed Wild Rice, Bacon
    & Cherries, 122
Honey-Soy Lamb & Rice, 119
Hummus
    Blanched Green Bean
        Salad, 139

I

Ingredients, storing wisely, 19
Irish-Style Lamb Stew, 118
Italian sausage
    Sausage, Fennel &
        Chicken, 87

J

Jalapeño pepper
    Chicken Chili Verde
        over Rice, 86
    Jalapeño-Bacon Mac
        & Cheese, 130
    Tex-Mex Quinoa, 126

K

Kabocha squash
    Barbecue Kabocha
        Squash, 62
Kale
    Braised Quinoa, Kale &
        Summer Squash, 63
    Cherry, Apple &
        Kale Salad, 137
    Garlicky Chicken
        Kale Soup, 55
    Orange-Soy Kale Salad
        with Mushrooms, 138
Kidney beans
    Minestrone, 48
Korean-Style Short Ribs
    & Carrots, 115

L

Lamb
    Greek-Style Lamb Shoulder
        & Lemon Potatoes, 113
    Honey-Soy Lamb
        & Rice, 119
    Irish-Style Lamb Stew, 118
    Osso Buco, 116
    Spanish-Style Lamb
        Chops, 114
Leeks
    Cream of Fennel &
        Leek Soup, 41
    Rutabaga & Sweet Potato
        Soup with Garlicky
        Ground Walnuts, 46
Lemon
    Chicken & Artichoke
        Bake, 81
    Garlicky Chicken
        Kale Soup, 55
    Greek-Style Lamb Shoulder
        & Lemon Potatoes, 113
    Lemon & Herb Barley
        Risotto, 123

Lentils
    Lentil, Chickpea & White
        Bean Stew, 58
    Rosemary Cauliflower
        & Lentils, 64
    Sweet Spiced Lentil
        Soup, 42
Lime
    Cuban-Style Pork
        Street Tacos, 98
    Gingery Quinoa
        Chicken, 127
List, shopping with a, 19
Low Calorie, 14

M

Mangos
    Chicken in Mango
        Chutney, 82
    Yogurt with Mangos
        & Cardamom, 29
Measurement conversions, 149
Meatloaf, 105
Mediterranean Couscous, 141
Milk. *See* Almond milk;
        Coconut milk
Minestrone, 48
Mixed Bean Chili, 65
Moroccan-Style Chickpeas
        with Chard, 67
Mozzarella cheese
    Chicken & Artichoke
        Bake, 81
    Roasted Red Pepper &
        Mozzarella Stuffed
        Chicken Breasts, 88
Mushrooms
    Beef Goulash with
        Pumpkin, Mushrooms
        & Pumpkin Seeds, 107
    Chicken with Mushrooms
        & Shallots, 83

Coq au Vin Blanc, 90
Mushroom Soup, 40
Orange-Soy Kale Salad
    with Mushrooms, 138
Spiced Pot Roast with
    Celery & Mushrooms, 112
Spinach, Mushroom
    & Swiss Cheese
    Crustless Quiche, 69
Vegetable Curry Soup, 52
Wild Mushroom
    Risotto, 124

N

Navy beans
    Cassoulet, 91
    Vegetarian Cassoulet, 77
Nutrition labels, 12–14

O

Oats
    Cinnamon Raisin
        Steel-Cut Oatmeal, 22
    Pear Chai-Spiced
        Oatmeal, 23
    Pumpkin Spice Oatmeal, 24
Olives
    Mediterranean
        Couscous, 141
Onions. *See also* Pearl
        onions; Red onions
    Adobo Steak Fajitas, 117
    Chicken Fajitas, 89
    Chicken Pot Pie, 85
    Minestrone, 48
    Pork Chops with Apples
        & Onions, 94
    Pot Roast, 108
    Shepherd's Pie, 104
Orange
    Cuban-Style Pork
        Street Tacos, 98

Orange-Soy Kale Salad
    with Mushrooms, 138
Osso Buco, 116

P

Parmesan cheese
    Ground Beef–Stuffed
        Bell Peppers, 106
    Ham & Cheese Breakfast
        Casserole, 34
Parsnips
    Creamy Butternut Squash
        & Parsnip Soup, 39
    Irish-Style Lamb Stew, 118
    Rosemary Parsnip
        Bisque with Toasted
        Bread Crumbs, 44
Peaches
    Chicken in Mango
        Chutney, 82
    Pork Tenderloin with
        Rosemary Peaches, 95
Peanut butter
    Spicy Peanut Rice Bake, 76
Peanuts
    Spicy Peanut Rice Bake, 76
Pear Chai-Spiced Oatmeal, 23
Pearl onions
    Coq au Vin Blanc, 90
Peas. *See also* Black-eyed
        peas; Chickpeas;
        Sugar snap peas
    Chicken Pot Pie, 85
    Shepherd's Pie, 104
    Split Pea Soup, 43
    Tempeh Shepherd's Pie, 72
Pepper Jack cheese
    Southwest Breakfast
        Casserole, 35
    Tempeh-Stuffed Bell
        Peppers, 73

Peppers. *See* Bell peppers; Jalapeño peppers
Pesto Chicken with Stewed Vegetables, 84
Plum tomatoes
    Barley Primavera, 129
    Beef Ragù, 111
    Blanched Green Bean Salad, 139
    Braised Quinoa, Kale & Summer Squash, 63
    Mediterranean Couscous, 141
    Quinoa Ratatouille Casserole, 125
    Simple Salad, 134
    Tofu Red Curry with Green Beans, 74
Pork
    Balsamic-Glazed Pork Tenderloin & Carrots, 96
    Carnitas with Avocado, Cilantro & Queso Fresco, 101
    Cranberry-Glazed PorkTenderloin, 100
    Cuban-Style Pork Street Tacos, 98
    Pork Chops with Apples & Onions, 94
    Pork Chops with Mashed Sweet Potatoes, 99
    Pork Tenderloin with Rosemary Peaches, 95
    Soy-Ginger Pork Chops with Green Beans, 97
Potatoes
    Baked Potato Soup, 47
    Chicken Pot Pie, 85
    Corn & Potato Chowder, 51
    Corn & Red Pepper Chowder, 45

Cream of Fennel & Leek Soup, 41
Ginger Carrot Bisque, 38
Greek-Style Lamb Shoulder & Lemon Potatoes, 113
Irish-Style Lamb Stew, 118
Pot Roast, 108
Prosciutto, Rosemary & Potato Breakfast Casserole, 33
Shepherd's Pie, 104
Smoked Salmon & Potato Casserole, 32
Spanish-Style Lamb Chops, 114
Tempeh Shepherd's Pie, 72
Pot Roast, 108
Prosciutto. *See also* Ham
    Prosciutto, Rosemary & Potato Breakfast Casserole, 33
Pumpkin
    Beef Goulash with Pumpkin, Mushrooms & Pumpkin Seeds, 107
    Pumpkin Black Bean Chili, 53
    Pumpkin Spice Oatmeal, 24

Q

Quiche, Spinach, Mushroom & Swiss Cheese Crustless, 69
Quinoa
    Braised Quinoa, Kale & Summer Squash, 63
    Breakfast Quinoa & Fruit, 25
    Cherry-Studded Quinoa Porridge, 26
    Gingery Quinoa Chicken, 127

Quinoa Ratatouille Casserole, 125
Tex-Mex Quinoa, 126

R

Raisins
    Cinnamon Raisin Steel-Cut Oatmeal, 22
Red bell peppers. *See also* Roasted red peppers
    Barley Primavera, 129
    Black Bean, Pepper & Corn Salad, 143
    Cuban-Style Pork Street Tacos, 98
    Ground Beef–Stuffed Bell Peppers, 106
    Pesto Chicken with Stewed Vegetables, 84
    Tempeh-Stuffed Bell Peppers, 73
    Vegetable Curry Soup, 52
Red cabbage
    Balsamic-Glazed Beef with Red Cabbage, 110
Red Curry Butternut Squash Soup, 50
Red onions
    Barbecue Kabocha Squash, 62
    Cuban-Style Pork Street Tacos, 98
Red wine
    Beef Ragù, 111
    Osso Buco, 116
    Spicy Mediterranean Beef Stew with Pearl Barley, 59
Rice. *See also* Brown rice; Wild rice
    Wild Mushroom Risotto, 124

Rice noodles
  Chilled Rice Noodle
    Salad, 142
Risotto
  Lemon & Herb Barley
    Risotto, 123
  Wild Mushroom
    Risotto, 124
Roasted red peppers
  Corn & Red Pepper
    Chowder, 45
  Roasted Red Pepper &
    Mozzarella Stuffed
    Chicken Breasts, 88
  Southwest Sweet Potato
    & Corn Scramble, 31
Rosemary
  Black-Eyed Peas with
    Rosemary, 144
  Pork Tenderloin with
    Rosemary Peaches, 95
  Prosciutto, Rosemary
    & Potato Breakfast
    Casserole, 33
  Rosemary Cauliflower
    & Lentils, 64
  Rosemary Parsnip
    Bisque with Toasted
    Bread Crumbs, 44
Rutabaga & Sweet Potato
  Soup with Garlicky
  Ground Walnuts, 46

S

Salads
  Black Bean, Pepper &
    Corn Salad, 143
  Blanched Green Bean
    Salad, 139
  Cherry, Apple &
    Kale Salad, 137

Chilled Rice Noodle
  Salad, 142
Orange-Soy Kale Salad
  with Mushrooms, 138
Simple Salad, 134
Spinach Salad with Figs
  & Walnuts, 136
Salmon, Smoked, & Potato
  Casserole, 32
Sausage, Fennel & Chicken, 87
Seitan
  Butter Seitan &
    Chickpeas, 71
  Seitan Tikka Masala, 70
Shallots, Chicken with
  Mushrooms &, 83
Shepherd's Pie, 104
Sides
  Black Bean, Pepper &
    Corn Salad, 143
  Black-Eyed Peas with
    Rosemary, 144
  Blanched Green Bean
    Salad, 139
  Cherry, Apple &
    Kale Salad, 137
  Chilled Rice Noodle
    Salad, 142
  Cilantro Rice Pilaf, 140
  Corn Bread, 147
  Fluffy Buttermilk
    Biscuits, 146
  Herbed Cucumbers, 135
  Mediterranean
    Couscous, 141
  Orange-Soy Kale Salad
    with Mushrooms, 138
  Simple Salad, 134
  Spinach Salad with Figs
    & Walnuts, 136
  Whole-Grain Dinner
    Rolls, 145

Simple Salad, 134
Slow cooker
  choosing a, 15
  food safety with, 14
  health benefits of
    using, 14–15
  healthy ingredients for, 18
  importance of for healthy
    meals, 12–14
  shopping and storage
    tips, 19
  smart planning for
    success, 15–16
  tips and tricks for
    delicious meals, 16–17
Smoked Salmon & Potato
  Casserole, 32
Socket trimer, 16
Soups
  Baked Potato Soup, 47
  Beef Barley Soup, 57
  Chicken Fajita Soup, 56
  Chicken Noodle Soup, 54
  Chipotle Black Bean
    Soup, 49
  Corn & Potato Chowder, 51
  Corn & Red Pepper
    Chowder, 45
  Cream of Fennel &
    Leek Soup, 41
  Creamy Butternut Squash
    & Parsnip Soup, 39
  Garlicky Chicken
    Kale Soup, 55
  Ginger Carrot Bisque, 38
  Irish-Style Lamb Stew, 118
  Minestrone, 48
  Mushroom Soup, 40
  Pumpkin Black
    Bean Chili, 53
  Red Curry Butternut
    Squash Soup, 50

Soups (*continued*)
Rosemary Parsnip
Bisque with Toasted
Bread Crumbs, 44
Rutabaga & Sweet Potato
Soup with Garlicky
Ground Walnuts, 46
Split Pea Soup, 43
Sweet Spiced Lentil
Soup, 42
Vegetable Curry Soup, 52
Southwest Breakfast
Casserole, 35
Southwest Sweet Potato &
Corn Scramble, 31
Southwestern Rice
Casserole, 131
Soy-Ginger Pork Chops with
Green Beans, 97
Spanish-Style Lamb Chops, 114
Spiced Pot Roast with Celery
& Mushrooms, 112
Spicy Peanut Rice Bake, 76
Spicy Mediterranean
Beef Stew with
Pearl Barley, 59
Spinach
Spinach & Black Bean
Enchilada Pie, 68
Spinach, Mushroom
& Swiss Cheese
Crustless Quiche, 69
Spinach Salad with Figs
& Walnuts, 136
Split Pea Soup, 43
Squash. *See* Butternut squash;
Kabocha squash;
Summer squash
Stew
Irish-Style Lamb Stew, 118
Lentil, Chickpea & White
Bean Stew, 58

Spicy Mediterranean
Beef Stew with
Pearl Barley, 59
Stir-Fry, Tofu, 75
Strawberry Cream Cheese
French Toast, 27
Sugar snap peas
Cashew Chicken &
Snap Peas, 92
Summer Squash, Braised
Quinoa, Kale &, 63
Sweet potato
Barbecue Kabocha
Squash, 62
Curried Sweet Potatoes
with Broccoli &
Cashews, 66
Pork Chops with Mashed
Sweet Potatoes, 99
Rutabaga & Sweet Potato
Soup with Garlicky
Ground Walnuts, 46
Southwest Sweet Potato
& Corn Scramble, 31
Wild Rice & Sweet
Potatoes, 128
Sweet Spiced Lentil Soup, 42
Swiss chard
Moroccan-Style Chickpeas
with Chard, 67
Swiss Cheese, Spinach,
Mushroom &,
Crustless Quiche, 69

T

Tempeh
Tempeh Shepherd's Pie, 72
Tempeh-Stuffed Bell
Peppers, 73
Tex-Mex Quinoa, 126
Tofu

Tofu Red Curry with
Green Beans, 74
Tofu Stir-Fry, 75
Tomatillos
Chicken Chili Verde
over Rice, 86
Tomatoes. *See also*
Fire-roasted tomatoes;
Plum tomatoes
Chicken & Artichoke
Bake, 81
Chicken Tikka Masala, 93
Minestrone, 48
Tortilla chips
Chicken Fajita Soup, 56
Tortillas
Adobo Steak Fajitas, 117
Carnitas with Avocado,
Cilantro & Queso
Fresco, 101
Chicken Fajitas, 89
Cuban-Style Pork
Street Tacos, 98
Southwest Breakfast
Casserole, 35
Spinach & Black Bean
Enchilada Pie, 68
Turkey
Meatloaf, 105

V

Veal
Osso Buco, 116
Vegan sausage
Vegetarian Cassoulet, 77
Vegetable broth
Balsamic-Glazed Pork
Tenderloin & Carrots, 96
Barbecue Kabocha
Squash, 62
Barley Primavera, 129

Braised Quinoa, Kale &
Summer Squash, 63
Chipotle Black Bean
Soup, 49
Creamy Butternut Squash
& Parsnip Soup, 39
Lemon & Herb Barley
Risotto, 123
Lentil, Chickpea & White
Bean Stew, 58
Minestrone, 48
Quinoa Ratatouille
Casserole, 125
Rosemary Cauliflower
& Lentils, 64
Rutabaga & Sweet Potato
Soup with Garlicky
Ground Walnuts, 46
Seitan Tikka Masala, 70
Southwestern Rice
Casserole, 131
Soy-Ginger Pork Chops
with Green Beans, 97
Spicy Peanut Rice Bake, 76
Sweet Spiced Lentil
Soup, 42
Tofu Red Curry with
Green Beans, 74
Vegetarian Cassoulet, 77
Wild Mushroom
Risotto, 124
Vegetable Curry Soup, 52
Vegetarian & Vegan Dishes
Barbecue Kabocha
Squash, 62
Braised Quinoa, Kale &
Summer Squash, 63

Butter Seitan &
Chickpeas, 71
Curried Sweet Potatoes
with Broccoli &
Cashews, 66
Mixed Bean Chili, 65
Moroccan-Style Chickpeas
with Chard, 67
Rosemary Cauliflower
& Lentils, 64
Seitan Tikka Masala, 70
Spicy Peanut Rice Bake, 76
Spinach & Black Bean
Enchilada Pie, 68
Spinach, Mushroom
& Swiss Cheese
Crustless Quiche, 69
Tempeh Shepherd's Pie, 72
Tempeh-Stuffed Bell
Peppers, 73
Tofu Red Curry with
Green Beans, 74
Tofu Stir-Fry, 75
Vegetarian Cassoulet, 77

W
Walnuts
Rutabaga & Sweet Potato
Soup with Garlicky
Ground Walnuts, 46
Spinach Salad with Figs
& Walnuts, 136
White beans
Lentil, Chickpea & White
Bean Stew, 58
White wine
Coq au Vin Blanc, 90

Whole-grain bread
Banana Nut French
Toast, 28
Ham & Cheese Breakfast
Casserole, 34
Spinach, Mushroom
& Swiss Cheese
Crustless Quiche, 69
Strawberry Cream Cheese
French Toast, 27
Whole-Grain Dinner Rolls, 145
Wild Mushroom Risotto, 124
Wild rice
Herbed Wild Rice, Bacon
& Cherries, 122
Wild Rice & Sweet
Potatoes, 128
Wine. *See* Red wine;
White wine

Y
Yeast
Whole-Grain Dinner
Rolls, 145
Yogurt
Corn Bread, 147
Yogurt & Berry Parfait, 30
Yogurt with Mangos
& Cardamom, 29

Z
Zucchini
Barley Primavera, 129
Pesto Chicken with
Stewed Vegetables, 84
Quinoa Ratatouille
Casserole, 125

CPSIA information can be obtained
at www.ICGtesting.com
Printed in the USA
LVOW06s1627131217
R13008100002B/R13008IPG559208LVX2B/1/P